HOW
I WRITE

Writers on Their Craft

HOW
I WRITE

Edited by
SONIA FALEIRO

HarperCollins *Publishers* India

First published in India by HarperCollins *Publishers* 2024
4th Floor, Tower A, Building No. 10, DLF Cyber City,
DLF Phase II, Gurugram, Haryana – 122002
www.harpercollins.co.in

2 4 6 8 10 9 7 5 3 1

P-ISBN: 978-93-6569-492-5
E-ISBN: 978-93-6569-489-5

Typeset in 12/16 Adobe Garamond at
HarperCollins *Publishers* India

Printed and bound at
Replika Press Pvt. Ltd.

To Pankaj Mishra, for your friendship,
unwavering support of South Asian writing,
and for leading by example.

CONTENTS

INTRODUCTION

In the summer of 2020, as the world retreated indoors, I found myself confined to a London apartment, poring over the proofs of my new book. The work—a deeply reported investigation into the deaths of two young girls in Uttar Pradesh—demanded my full attention. Yet, even as I combed through the pages for errors, I was acutely aware of the support that had buoyed me through the complexities of the project. My family, close friends, agent, editors and a small circle of writerly confidants had all played crucial roles in steering me through a book that was as challenging as it was necessary.

It was during those prolonged, reflective hours that the notion of South Asia Speaks began to take shape. The pandemic, while contracting the world, had also highlighted the essential nature of community—a web of support I felt compelled to offer to fellow writers. Friends in the literary sphere—Prayaag Akbar, Rahul Bhatia, Fatima Bhutto, Isaac Chotiner, McKenzie Funk, Samar Halarnkar, Marc Herman, Aruni Kashyap, Mira Kamdar, Nikita Lalwani, Aanchal Malhotra, Sanam Maher, Karan Mahajan, Mahesh Rao, Arunava Sinha, Samanth Subramanian, Altaf Tyrewala, Madhuri Vijay and Mirza Waheed—shared my concern, and together, we resolved to act by fostering a new generation of literary talent.

The timing of our launch was no accident. South Asia was, and continues to be, a region where freedom of expression is increasingly under siege. Journalists, writers and artists are being silenced, and the truth has become a perilous thing to tell. In this climate, our goal became clear: to provide a platform for writers whose stories are essential to understanding the realities of South Asia. Our fellows' debut publications, including by Zeyad Masroor Khan, by Nusrat F. Jafri and by Shah Tazrian Ashrafi, are a testament to this mission. We also agreed to elevate voices traditionally excluded from mainstream publishing—not just to correct historical wrongs, but because these voices bring a much-needed freshness and urgency to contemporary literature. Each new cohort is a reflection of the rich diversity and complexity of South Asian culture and society.

By 2021, South Asia Speaks had taken shape as an organization dedicated to offering emerging South Asian writers the kind of backing my colleagues and I had been fortunate enough to receive. It would offer an annual fellowship for unpublished writers from South Asia who were engaged in substantial projects—whether in fiction, non-fiction, reportage, translation or poetry. Each September, an invitation for applications would go out, and selected writers would then be paired with mentors—established authors who would guide them through the labyrinth of the writing process, from pitching to submission.

The approach worked. Now nearing its fifth year, the initiative has become a beacon for promising literary voices across the region. To date, South Asia Speaks writers have published more than half a dozen books, secured scholarships to prestigious programmes like the Iowa Writers' Workshop and the Logan Nonfiction Program, and won accolades from the PEN/Heim Translation Fund, the International Women in Media Foundation and the New India Foundation, among others.

We have also continued to grow. In 2022, South Asia Speaks expanded its offerings with a series of masterclasses featuring some of the world's most respected writers. These sessions, which are the interviews in this book, have evolved beyond their initial purpose of inspiring our fellows. Our next initiative, Beyond Ability, launched in 2023, reflects our commitment to inclusivity. Helmed by the disabled writer Abhishek Annica, this fellowship is designed specifically for writers who identify as having a disability. In 2024, we introduced workshops on craft, led by distinguished mentors like Diksha Basu, Taymour Soomro and Roman Gautam. All these opportunities are provided at no cost to our fellows, as we firmly believe that financial barriers should never hinder creative potential.

The South Asia Speaks Masterclass series, which you now hold in your hands, was conceived as a space for the most important writers of South Asian origin to speak candidly about their craft. These writers have won the highest accolades in publishing, yet their voices are often overshadowed by discussions of their cultural backgrounds rather than their creative processes. What began as a resource for our fellows has evolved into something much more: a deep, introspective exploration of what it means to be a creative person navigating and responding to a tumultuous world. It is also a heartfelt conversation, filled with warmth and wisdom.

This collection is by no means exhaustive—such a task would be impossible given the vast linguistic, cultural and geographical expanse of South Asia. The writers included are those we admire and who also generously agreed to share their insights with our fellows at no cost. Figures like Pankaj Mishra, Kamila Shamsie, Manjushree Thapa, V.V. Ganeshananthan, Mira Nair and Jamal Jan Kochai, among others, waived their fees for these masterclasses. Thanks to them, every sale of this book will directly benefit South Asia Speaks, allowing us to continue supporting the next generation of South Asian literary talent. For this act of solidarity, I extend my deepest gratitude.

At the heart of every masterclass is a simple, yet profound, question: How did you do it? The answers are as varied as the writers themselves. Pankaj Mishra recounts a chance encounter in a Delhi hotel that led to a career-defining relationship with *The New York Review of Books*. Mayukh Sen shares the burden of confronting racism and envy as a young, brown-skinned food writer. V.V. Ganeshananthan reveals how she navigated the physical challenges posed by her motor disability to write her Women's Prize–winning novel. And filmmaker Mira Nair speaks about the irreplaceable value of creative community—a principle we, at South Asia Speaks, hold dear.

Each masterclass has offered me new insights and unexpected joys. My hope is that this collection will do the same for you. Thank you for supporting this book and, in turn, the future of South Asian literature.

Sonia Faleiro
London, 2024

PANKAJ MISHRA

INTERVIEWED BY

SONIA FALEIRO

❧

'You have to be very clear
about who you're standing in
solidarity with'

SONIA FALEIRO (SF): Pankaj, may I ask what drew you to books?

PANKAJ MISHRA (PM): What drew me to books was the experience of living in very small places where there was really nothing to feed the imagination. There was no television, obviously; there was some cinema, there was the radio and then there were books—randomly read, picked up here and there. In that kind of almost completely distraction-free environment, books were the most reliable guarantor of information, analysis, mental stimulation and excitement. So, I started reading very early, and I was a very precocious reader, because I would read whatever was available. That meant even serious books that I didn't entirely understand; in fact, I didn't understand most of what I was reading. But nevertheless, I was reading.

And then as I grew up, there was a feeling crystallizing inside me, that what I really wanted was to continue the life that I had as a child, which was a life of freedom, of reading, thinking and writing. I had no idea, to be honest, how to go about creating such an existence. The idea of becoming a writer was very distant; it was not a widely embraced aspiration. Fortunately enough, the future worked out, and I was able to do what I wanted.

SF: Were there writers in your family?

PM: There were writers in the sense that there were people who went home after a long and tiring day and wrote a piece of poetry, a short story, or an essay, but nobody who could claim to be a published writer. They were people who published a few things here and there in the newspapers or magazines, my father was one of them, but they hadn't done so consistently enough to claim that they were writers, and they certainly hadn't published books.

SF: So, when you came up with the idea of becoming a writer, which was unusual for its time, how did your family react?

PM: Nobody supported me by saying, 'Okay, I really like what you're doing. Perhaps you should continue to do this.' But there was something more important than support, in at least my context, which was an attitude of, broadly speaking, tolerance, like, 'We are not going to raise serious objections to the path you have set out on, which is a highly unconventional path.' I can't tell you how valuable that was. To have my parents and siblings, and, indeed, other people think or say, 'Okay, let's see what comes of this', rather than saying, as was the case with many people I knew, 'How are you going to make a living?' That was a very serious question to which there were no clear answers back then— there still aren't. How are you going to make a living as a journalist, writer, novelist—these are still questions we haven't resolved, not only in India, but in some of the richer societies of the world.

SF: Your new novel *Run and Hide* (Penguin, 2023) like your first novel *The Romantics* (Knopf, 2000) is about caste and class. Did these elements shape your early years?

PM: The older I grow, the more I realize that the first twenty years of my existence still remain the most valuable, in the sense of the varieties of lives, classes and places they exposed me to. My father worked for the railways, so we moved around quite a lot. I was exposed to the cruelties that people of a higher caste inflict on people from a lower caste; I was exposed to the communal poison of Hindu supremacists expressing nasty views about Muslims, Sikhs and Christians. My family was full of Hindu right-wingers—it still is—and that, again, was a very valuable experience in the long term. But, of course, at the time there was no hope of the Hindu nationalists ever coming to power, so most of us regarded them with mockery.

Those experiences made me, and forged my material, something that I'm still working with thirty years later, and will probably continue to work with. Once you've had a fundamental experience of social disparity, caste injustice or class cruelties, then you can see them in a wide variety of contexts, as opposed to being largely oblivious to them, which is, I'm afraid, the case with many people who live in Europe and America, who are shielded from these realities because those societies have done an excellent job of disguising cruelty and injustice.

SF: You studied at the University of Allahabad and then moved to Benaras. What did your experience of college politics tell you about who we are and what we might become?

PM: The University of Allahabad was an extremely interesting place. It was already in decline, and had been taken over by an anarchic, violent form of student politics—people were literally shooting at each other on campus. Intense rivalries erupted all the time, and I was often witness to these existential battles. It was a very important lesson in politics in our part of the world, which is that politics is not merely a battle for power, it is a battle for survival, and often one person's existence is a direct challenge to the survival of the other, so someone has to die.

I then moved to Benares where it was much more intense, because the stakes were higher; Benares is an important political constituency, it's not surprising that Narendra Modi chose to contest from it. It was also full of anarchist violence, and I came to know people who were perpetrating it and who were also its victims. These were people who came from lower-class backgrounds, often from extremely poor families, who had come to the provincial university to make careers for themselves, but then got sucked into student politics. Living amidst these extremely violent battles, often between different caste groups—Thakurs, Brahmins, Boomihars—was a routine thing. I was left with few illusions about the state of Indian democracy, specifically the claim of a peaceful transfer of power every five years. I could never really make those claims because the reality I had seen was very different, and, in many cases, it has become much worse.

One reason why journalism has been in crisis for such a long time is because we have lost touch with many of the realities out there, and it's only very recently, in the last ten years or so, that we've had people covering these areas consistently and writing about the social pathologies that exist there—the weird mix of a consumption-oriented modernity, and really squalid superstitions and prejudices. That's the world I was thrown into back then, and I remember those years with some relief that I survived them personally, but also with some gratitude that I was able to experience those realities before they became distant from me.

SF: Did being in the midst of all that make you want to escape?

PM: Oh, absolutely! Back then, dealing with that kind of thing, fearing for my life—not only for my life but wondering at what point I might lose a limb or two in the battles—and the general sense of despair and failure that hung over the place made me want to put it behind me. At that point though, I didn't have the resources to do anything else apart from go and live in a village. Of course, there was an in-between period when I studied at JNU, which was a really wonderful interlude.

I left JNU while I was still a student, and went to Himachal where I found a place in a little village, which I still have, and there I started to live and write reviews. The head of Penguin India read some of my reviews and asked if I would like to write a book. I accepted extremely eagerly, without knowing what I was going to write about. I said, 'Sure, why not? Let's do a travel book.' I'd never thought of writing a travel book but the idea that I could actually publish a book was so overwhelming that I took up the offer. I travelled around, and then wrote *Butter Chicken in Ludhiana* (Penguin, 1995). I was twenty-four, and it obviously reads like a young person's book, but that experience of travelling through small-town India was extremely valuable. It exposed me to the realities that had begun to be very apparent back in the mid 90s: the aggressive Hindutva-driven politics, the prejudices openly expressed against Muslims, and the aspiration that India was going to be a superpower and that everyone was going to be rich.

SF: Was this when you started writing for *The New York Review of Books*?

PM: That came not long after I published the travel book. The editor Barbara Epstein was visiting Delhi—I got to know about this from the papers—and I knew that she had personally known Edmund Wilson whom I was very interested in writing about. So, I rang The Claridges Hotel and asked to speak to her. I said, 'I really would like to speak to you, if only on the phone, about Edmund Wilson', and she said, 'Why on the phone? Come to the hotel for tea tomorrow', and so I went over and had tea. She asked me what I did and what I had written and I told her, and she said, 'Oh my goodness! That book was literally recommended to me two hours ago by (the Italian journalist) Tiziano Terzani. And what are you writing these days?' I said, 'Actually, the reason why I met you is because I want to write an article about reading Edmund Wilson in Benares and I want to know what kind of person he was.' She said, 'Well, when you finish that piece, send it to me.' So, I sent it to her more than a year later, and she sent a fax back saying, 'We'd love to carry this.' And that, for a writer who'd just started out, was fantastic news, as you can imagine.

SF: Your pieces in *The New York Review of Books* shaped how people outside saw India, particularly how they saw contested areas such as Kashmir and the Naxal territory. Can you talk to me about the choices that you made and how they were received?

PM: In India they were met with hostility for the most part, especially the pieces on Kashmir, because the national ideology at the time—which journalists also subscribed to—was that Kashmiris had to be saved from themselves, that Indian secularism was the way forward and that reports of atrocities committed on Kashmiris by the Indian military were unhelpful. I think that was the broad response to my pieces, which were attacked, often viciously.

From that first moment when I was made to feel marginalized, I actually felt completely free. I did not have to subscribe to the dominant orthodoxy in India—and later on in the West—I could follow my own instincts. And my instincts were that of the novelist inside me, because a novelist is always interested in the fate of individuals. And when that individual is suffering, that is what you respond to. I was approaching my subjects with the kind of empathetic intelligence that a novelist brings, feeling a high degree of sympathy with the people who were being victimized. I've never really departed from that fundamental way of looking at journalism; in the end, who are you really responsible for? What is your analytical framework? What should shape your narrative, if not sympathy with the underdog?

To this day, I cannot understand journalists who write in praise of Modi, or Imran Khan or Joe Biden. What are you doing, writing in praise of the powerful? What you really should be doing is describing the experiences of the powerless. You have to be very clear in your mind about who you're standing in solidarity with.

SF: Does a writer's commitment need to extend beyond the page?

PM: I think journalism can and should be a form of activism. But it's a long-term form of activism, in the sense that one is already performing a service by being an eyewitness and reporting as accurately as possible. That testimony grows more important over time, other people are going to build on it, draw inspiration from it, and use it in their own works. So, it's a form of political activism on behalf of truth. The loss of trust in the media has been one of the most disturbing symptoms of democratic decline over the last decade or so, and that's what makes journalism so much more valuable.

SF: You were one of the few people who warned against electing Narendra Modi. I know that you faced a great deal of harassment as a result. Can you talk about that?

PM: I can tell you honestly that the months before, and immediately after, the 2014 election in India formed the worst period in my life, because of the delusion that had overwhelmed some of the best minds. The delusion that Narendra Modi was a saviour and would finally make India the international superpower that previous governments had failed to. I just could not believe that often highly intelligent people believed the rubbish that we now know to be propaganda. It was a terrible moment—not finding allies—and then, of course, in the West, apart from a few exceptions, most people were excited as well because Modi was seen as a free-marketeering incarnation of Ronald Reagan or Margaret Thatcher, who was finally going to introduce the reforms that media like *The Wall Street Journal* had long been arguing for.

Then, of course, Modi won, and his victory was seen as a vindication of all these hopes. In the bleak years since 2014, we've seen many such victories—whether it's Donald Trump or Brexit or [Viktor] Orbán in Hungary—and we now know how people can be persuaded to vote in truly monstrous figures. In the end, I think, you have to stick to your principles. It was always incredibly unlikely that a man whose only real achievement was in PR, was going to be an effective Prime Minister of India, and it didn't take long for that to be proved. Now most people are saying, 'We don't want to be a part of this', but it's too late, unfortunately.

SF: Anybody writing critically of Modi is not just being trolled, but is also in danger of being arrested. What kind of advice would you give writers who want to report the truth but are understandably concerned for their safety?

PM: What's really disturbing to me is the way that people like Modi and other autocrats around the world are creating digital fortresses in which they unleash their troll armies and disinformation troopers on the very tiny group of journalists who are trying to do their job. In terms of how one deals with it, well, one can only go on writing and reporting the truth as rigorously as possible. As far as publishing is concerned, we need to create other sources and find receptive audiences outside South Asia. What you're doing with South Asia Speaks ties up very well with this, because it is bringing the enormous pool of talent that exists in South Asia in contact with people outside, so that the feeling of suffocation or hopelessness that many writers in South Asia may have today is somewhat alleviated.

SF: I have to, of course, ask about V.S. Naipaul. What influence did he have on your career?

PM: Naipaul was hugely important to all of us who were writing, but had no resources to realize that particular ambition. The myth of Naipaul was that of someone who came out of nowhere and started to write, and finally became a writer who was widely celebrated. That myth was hugely important in the shaping of my own ambition.

But the thing about influence is that at some point you have to outgrow the people who mentor you and find your own path. That happens naturally when you become more confident. You discover new material and new ways of writing about that material. For instance, Naipaul's journalism is not something I would teach anyone because it's very lazy. He was a brilliant interviewer who got whatever people said right on the page—the way they looked, the way their offices looked. What he didn't do was put it in any kind of context. When he went to Iran, the year after the Shah was deposed, he only focused on how people turned into Islamic revolutionaries. What made them turn into Islamic revolutionaries wasn't at all covered. That is lazy journalism. You should be interested in the history of Iran, its economy and politics. Talking to individuals and thinking, 'Oh, this individual is quite neurotic, so neurosis must be at the basis of the Islamic revolution', is very shallow. It was important for me to break with that kind of journalism and to understand that if I'm approaching a society, I need to learn as much as possible about it. When I started to write about China, it took me three or four years of simply reading about China, and then travelling there multiple times before I felt, 'Okay, I now feel confident enough to write my first piece about this society.'

Naipaul was very poorly read in history, and he was very poorly read, generally, in many of the societies he wrote about. I think it's important to read up on other people who have gone before you and have done the hard work. You can't be arrogant in thinking that you're going to describe a society through personal interviews with people.

SF: I have been meaning to ask this question, which is that, because of the work that you do many people think you are incredibly serious—which you are—but people who know you, know that you also have an incredible sense of joy and fun, that you love your family and friends. I am keen to know how you maintain that balance.

PM: Oh, that's incredibly kind—I'm very touched. I think if you deal with bleak subjects, you need something to ground you. The only release I get from constantly writing about politically adverse situations is by spending time with friends and family. All of us feel, at some level, the sense that we are powerless, and that whatever we write has no power to change anything. So, we live with that sense of impotence in our writing. But where we do have a sense of agency, where we can make life better for ourselves and for other people, is in our everyday interactions. For me, the right formula is thinking, 'There's very little I can do about larger political situations. Where I can make a difference is that when somebody needs help or my company, I can provide it. I can be there for that person.'

MAYUKH SEN

INTERVIEWED BY

SANAM MAHER

~

'Dealing with the naked racism in this industry has been very taxing'

Sanam Maher (SM): Let's start by talking about when you first developed an interest in writing about food. Your first job was with the website Food52. What was it like writing about food at the time?

Mayukh Sen (MS): I was hired by Food52 in 2016 when I was twenty-four years old. An editor at Food52 found me and said, 'Hey, we are looking for a staff writer who can write about culture through the lens of food.' I was young and eager to find the trust of an editor who would allow me to write deeply reported stories, which was not easy for a young freelancer, especially from a marginalized community. I'm not a white dude, right?

I had come into it thinking that food writing was a genre with limited possibilities, in the sense that it was mostly about restaurant criticism, which was the domain of white, middle-class dudes. I also believed that it had to do with cooking and recipe development, which wasn't a skill I had. I knew I wanted to do something a little different, but it was tough, because when I got the job, I was the only person of colour on staff, which was composed entirely of white women. It was a wonderful collection of white women and I loved them dearly, but I was writing from a different centre of gravity in the sense that my food memories were of a Bengali immigrant household in New Jersey.

The way I found my footing in those early days was by writing a lot of personal essays, like about how fruitcake was a gastronomic and homophobic slur in the West,[1] one that I heard levelled against me a lot growing up. Many people called me 'fruitcake' before I even knew I was queer. But my Bengali family loved fruitcake. I ate it a lot and treasured it as a delicacy. It was one of the first essays that got me on people's radars and showed that I might have something critical to say about the American food media and its DNA. In that piece, I explored the two different meanings that fruitcake possesses in the cultural vernacular, and then talked about how the American food media had for so long presupposed a certain kind of reader, who was more likely to be white and had an 'American' palate. When you are assuming that of your audience, there are so many others who get excluded.

SM: That essay is such a great example of how food writing can be a vehicle to talk about an array of experiences. What kind of reception did you get?

MS: One of the biggest challenges was dealing with the readers. The implicit assumption was that our reader was a white woman in the American Midwest with conservative values. I was tasked with writing for her, which was a big challenge. It did, in some ways, force me to be a more precise writer, in the sense that if I wanted to say anything radical, I had to figure out a way to introduce it. My final feature for Food52 was a piece on Joyce Chen,[2] who was, as far as we know, the first woman of colour to host her own nationally syndicated cooking show on American TV. This was

---

1   Mayukh Sen, 'How—and Why—Did Fruitcake Become a Slur?', Food52, 22 December 2016.

2   Mayukh Sen, 'America's Forgotten Television Chef', Food52, 3 October 2017.

back in the 60s, right after Julia Child rose to fame through *The French Chef.* Joyce Chen was an immigrant from China and her show lasted a mere season. She didn't have the same longevity in American memory as Child has had. I wanted to resuscitate her story or at least restore some dignity to it.

The simple fact that she was the first woman of colour to host her own nationally syndicated cooking show in America rankled many readers. They said things like, 'I wish you hadn't mentioned she was the first woman of colour', and 'You should just focus on her accomplishments, why bring race into it?' There was this whole back and forth and some very impassioned defenders joined in the debate saying, 'He's stating a fact, this is not a controversial statement', and 'What is wrong with bringing a smidge of racial analysis to this piece, especially when analysing who gets written into certain histories, and who doesn't?' It was tough, and I had to prod my editors to step in and defend me in the comments.

Many people who read me were not a part of the core imagined audience at Food52; I wish I had thought about that with more diligence early in my career. After my father died I wrote a piece about what upper caste Bengali widows were forced to eat after their husband's death. In hindsight, I wish I had thought about what people in South Asia, broadly, and especially Bengalis, would have thought, as I was characterizing certain cultural practices within that piece. That is a question that I really started asking myself as I was writing my first book *Taste Makers: Seven Immigrant Women Who Revolutionized Food in America* (WW Norton, 2021) in order to unlearn the idea that my reader was always going to be a lady named Deborah in Wisconsin.

SM: You won the James Beard Award in 2018 when you were twenty-six years old. It has a lot of clout. What did it mean to you then, and what did it end up meaning?

MS: I'm really glad you outlined the difference. At the time, to be completely honest, it felt like the best and biggest thing to ever happen to me. It was beyond my wildest dreams and this is coming from someone who grew up watching the Oscars. I was like, 'I got my moment on an award stage!' I was a little dork, but I had also experienced a lot of hardship the prior year. I was harassed by commentators, then I lost my father to cancer, and then I went on to another job where I was dealing with some very challenging discriminatory situations. After those difficult experiences, to get this validation and affirmation was beyond what I had imagined. It felt wonderful, and I tried to let myself feel very happy.

It also opened up access to capital and opportunity that would not otherwise have been available to someone who looks like me. It put me in front of gatekeepers who respected me, whereas a few months before, they would probably have been like, 'Who's this brown child?' After I won I felt like I could sell a book that was along the same lines; in terms of exploring the stories of people who had been erased within the larger canon of American food history. But I do not conflate the recognition with confirmation of my talent.

I will say that I felt some resentment from older folks in the industry—people who have historically had a lot of power. They seemed upset that I had gotten the validation, and that resentment came out in very ugly ways that were challenging for me. Dealing with the naked racism in this industry has been very taxing.

SM: Can you talk about how the idea for the book came to be?

MS: In the summer of 2017, one of my writer friends, Shuja Haider, who is an editor at *The Nation*, was reading my work and said, 'Is there a project that stitches some of these stories together to tell a larger narrative about immigrants and food in America?' I was like, 'Huh, that's interesting.' But I was twenty-five and not mature enough to take on a book project. So, I kept the idea in my back pocket. Winning the James Beard Award in 2018 helped me feel more confident in my abilities. That's when I started to devote my time and energy to writing a proposal.

I noticed, just over the course of that year, so many narratives in the American food media that were along the lines of 'immigrants get the job done' and 'immigrants feed America'. To me, those talking points felt patronizing because they obscured the creative aspirations of immigrants and their actual labour, and reinforced the notion that the value of immigrant lives, at least within the American context, should be measured by their productivity and what they provide to a certain kind of consumer whom the American food media had privileged for so long—and that person was, as I mentioned earlier, white and middle class. I wanted to write against that and felt that the best way to do that was through posthumous profiles of immigrant women who had shaped food in America, and, for the most part, had not been given the respect they deserved.

SM: I read about how after you lost your dad you panicked about forgetting, and that fear fed into the process of writing this book. Do you want to talk about that?

MS: After my dad died in 2017, I started to forget his voice and how he had moved through the world—things that had been so familiar to me throughout my life. That was terrifying. I couldn't believe that I could forget, so easily, someone who had been such a vivid presence in my life. I felt as though writing was a way to combat that, and to at least try to cement his essence in a more permanent form, and ensure that some aspect of him lived on beyond his lifetime. That was the engine behind my project.

I was also thinking constantly about my mom, because I'm very fortunate to have a wonderful relationship with her and we've only grown closer since my father died. I talk to her every day. My mom grew up in a village called Balarampur in West Bengal, outside Kolkata, and had an arranged marriage. It was very tough for her to give up her family for a set of strangers, who, to say it charitably, did not treat her with the respect she deserved, and certainly did not respect her labour. That was the environment in which I grew up, one that just so casually and flagrantly disrespected everything my mother was doing to keep our unit alive. I was very close to her, and this injustice always angered me.

Writing my book allowed me to see this injustice in an even more complicated light, to understand the link between what goes on in homes like the one that I grew up in, and the larger cultural forces that are so willing and eager to erase or downplay the labour of women. Something I was thinking about a lot as I wrote *Taste Makers*, was the idea that women's cooking is often dismissed by cultural gatekeepers as not a true form of creative expression. I wanted to show that it is a form of creative expression that has value and meaning. I hope that my mom has seen aspects of her story as an immigrant woman reflected in my book.

SM: I want to talk a little bit about your decision to de-centre your own voice. How did that work?

MS: I had, by late 2018 when I sold the book, written many posthumous profiles that followed the same narrative beat. They started with a compelling enough lead and at the end of the first section they said, 'This is why you should care about this person but this is how she's been erased.' Then the narrative unspooled, and, at the end, it talked about how her legacy deserved more. I wanted to force myself out of the pattern of writing dinky little articles where I was inserting myself into the narrative through the first person. I wanted to cede the stage to the individual I was profiling, and in doing that to create a document that would age well.

There are many merits to directly quoting sources—you offer transparency to the reader, for example. I took a different approach, though I'm sure there'll be some readers of my book who'll be like, 'Where is he getting this information?' Unless you flip to the endnotes you're not going to see a direct source. I knew, in that sense, that my method was a risk, but it was a different experience for me and I hoped that it would be a different experience for my readers. I hope it allowed my readers to live inside the head of each of these women, because in the case of the posthumous profiles, I spent so much time with the women's memoirs, cookbooks and interviews, and felt a kinship with them. I wanted to convey that sense of intimacy on the page.

SM: I wonder how you feel about writing about your community under the white gaze. What I mean is that sometimes writing authentically about our communities requires a level of self-criticism, but can feel like betrayal when aired in front of a mainstream audience. How do you deal with that?

MS: The last thing I want is for anyone from a similar background to feel that I am scrubbing out the complications and nuances of our existence for mass consumption. If you look at my early work, you can probably see evidence of that, because that's just a part of what it means to be a writer of colour from a marginalized community writing in America today.

When I do write about Bengali food or Indian cinema or something like that, I try to make sure that my editor is well versed in the complications of our community so that they have my back, because I think so much can get lost when you're doing the work of translating to a wider audience. I want to make sure that my editor is keeping me in check and being like, 'No, you are doing this in a way that does a disservice to the community.' I try to make sure I am working with Indian-origin or South Asian-origin editors, or for publications that are Indian. The last thing that I want is for someone who is Bengali to be like, 'I hate the way in which you mischaracterized our people and where we come from, and the community to which you belong.' In cases like those, I care more about their sensitivities than the sensitivities of my non-Bengali readers.

SM: Can you talk about your writing process?

MS: I feel very privileged to be able to focus almost entirely on writing for a living. That is something my late father wanted to do and could not because of his circumstances, so it is a gift. I do experience anxiety and think, 'I hate my voice. I hate the way that it emerges on the page. I wish I wrote like this person or that person.'

I will be transparent with you. When I wrote the first draft of *Taste Makers* in 2019, I was sinking under a lot of challenges. As I said earlier, I was subject to really ugly attacks from gatekeepers in the food media, which demolished my spirits. Dealing with that was tough, and in addition to that—I say this because I trust you—I had a very bad relationship with alcohol and was drinking constantly. It was a really unhealthy rhythm. I've been sober now for two years and since then my process has looked different, in the sense that I am very conscientious of being alive outside of my book and my writing, and of making sure that I am consuming as much art as I can, because it makes me a better writer. It's easiest to write when I am not spending my free time on Twitter or Instagram, but instead watching a movie or spending time with a friend or reading. The whole adage of 'read more than you write' does hold true and is something that I try to follow as diligently as possible. When I was young and ambitious and got institutional recognition and validation, it was easy to be like, 'Wow! My life, my identity is of being a food writer with a James Beard Award.' That's pathetic and it leads to heartache and pain—at least it did for me—so what I tell my students and other writers is to make sure they have a life outside of writing. Ultimately, that makes you a better writer.

SM: Has teaching changed the way that you write?

MS: It certainly has. I started teaching in 2019, when I was going through personal stuff. Many of my students spoke English as a second language and had never taken a journalism or writing class. That forced me to teach them the basics. The process of relearning the fundamentals of building a story, of making sure the architecture and scaffolding were there, was really helpful for me.

That said, because teaching forces you to strip down to the fundamentals, you become a little more timid as a writer. When I revisit my early work, I feel as though I had a bit more whimsy on a sentence level; that I was willing to throw stuff at the wall and see what stuck. I worry that with *Taste Makers*, there's less of that; that it's very tight and rigid. I wish I had allowed myself to loosen up a bit more as I was writing. I hope that I can allow myself to have fun again because when you experience pleasure, your reader will too.

SM: I don't think it's rigid. I think there's so much feeling in the book. The last question I have is: How do you choose what's going to be your first book?

MS: I was very scared that if I tried to write a book that was not about food, not about women from marginalized communities— which is what I had been institutionally recognized for—that the book would not sell. To be completely honest, I was being strategic in saying, 'This is what I have gotten attention for from people who have capital, so I need to lean into it.' That's not to say that I don't care about those stories—I care about them deeply and what a gift it was to write the book, but I think I needed to say, 'What avenues will this open up for me to get even closer to my passions and interests?'

I grew up to be a film critic. I love writing about film, and it is what keeps me up at night. My second book is a biography of the old Hollywood star, Merle Oberon, who was born in Bombay and then lived in Calcutta for most of her childhood (*Love, Queenie: Merle Oberon, Hollywood's First South Asian Star*, WW Norton, 2025). In the 30s and 40s, Oberon became a huge star in British and American cinema, and was the first woman of colour to get an Oscar nomination for Best Actress in 1936. But throughout her lifetime she hid from the public the fact that her mother was partially Sri Lankan, and that she was brown. She passed for white. She was a trailblazer in a traditional sense that she broke a barrier, and was the first best actress nominee of Asian descent, but she also hid a crucial aspect of herself throughout her public life.

I am so excited to write this book. It is closer to what I want to write ultimately and what my passion is. I hope that I will look back on my career, decades from now, and see my Merle Oberon book as a step towards becoming the most fully formed writer I can possibly be.

KAMILA SHAMSIE

INTERVIEWED BY

SANAM MAHER

'No piece of writing is ever wasted'

Sanam Maher (SM): You once said that you have to look deep within yourself to find a story that matters. Let's start with that idea in the context of your new book, *Best of Friends* (Bloomsbury, 2022).

Kamila Shamsie (KS): It's a book I started in 2019. I was quite lucky that when Covid-19 happened, and we went into lockdown, I had a novel to work on. My plan for 2020 was to say no to everything and to chain myself to a desk and write, so that was that.

SM: You manifested it!

KS: The universe kind of swung in my direction! I'd wanted to write a novel with friendship at its centre, because friendship is such a central relationship in most people's lives—it certainly is in mine. I was irritated by the fact that there weren't enough novels about friendships; it was always a subplot. As I'm getting older, I'm particularly interested in relationships I have had since childhood. I don't even remember when my earliest friendship started. We were in a classroom together and then we were friends. Now we're turning fifty. I expect that the milestone made me think about friendship.

The other thing I was very aware of was about what happens when friends find themselves on different sides of a political divide. It happened with Brexit in Britain and Trump in America.

I have Indian friends who are divided over Narendra Modi and Pakistani friends who have differing opinions on Imran Khan. I've always been interested in how politics can be very deeply personal; decisions made in Islamabad or Westminster or DC inform what we do and don't have the freedom to do, and yet are often seen as separate. I wanted to collapse that distance.

In 2018, I was writing an article about the Pakistani women's cricket team and its history, which went back to December 1988, when two teenage sisters, Shaiza [Khan] and Sharmeen [Khan], who were Pakistani but were playing cricket for England when Benazir Bhutto was elected Prime Minister, thought, 'Well, if Pakistan can have a woman Prime Minister, it can have a women's cricket team.' They went to Karachi and organized a match at the National Stadium, between a team of women they put together and a men's side. And the religious parties who had just been decimated in the elections wanted to show that they still had street power, so they staged massive protests, and the match was called off.

As I was writing about December 1988, I felt this sort of cracking in my spine and thought, 'Why have I never written about what it was to be a teenager in that moment?' At that point I located something specific, which is that the novel was going to start around the period in Pakistan's history when Bhutto became Prime Minister.

SM: So, you had a swirl of ideas. What came next?

KS: Once I had a time and place—Karachi, 1988, I knew something about the atmosphere of change and possibility, and I knew there would be two girls. With every novel there are certain gifts that come your way, and the gift with this one was that I didn't have to work very hard to know the friends; I recognized their friendship early on. I sat with these characters, and little moments and images came to me, and then I had a starting point.

History proved quite useful. (General) Zia died in early August 1988, which is just after the beginning of the school term, and Bhutto was voted to power in December, which is near the end of the school term. I knew very early that the first half of the novel would take place within a single school term, so I had a bounded space. One of the important things to do with writing is to narrow things down; there's nothing worse than the 'anything could happen anywhere with anyone' scenario.

Then, I started to write and it's actually the writing that, for me, engenders ideas. I'm going to read out this line which I found a while ago, which is me saying, 'Writing is a process of dealing with not knowing, a forcing of what and how; the not knowing is crucial to art, it is what permits art to be made. Without the scanning process engendered by not knowing, without the possibility of having the mind move in unanticipated directions, there would be no invention.' And there's something in there that I really love. That idea that if you don't know what's going to come next, your brain is scanning ahead and looking at all these different possibilities and constantly surprising itself.

SM: I understand you're very comfortable with the fact that your first drafts are messy.

KS: If anyone ever asks me one piece of advice for writers, it's always, 'Get to the end of your first draft.' Don't worry about making it good. There needs to be enough there for you to work with, and if I didn't know I could revise, I'd be paralysed with fear—I'd never be able to write anything. The first draft is where I'm feeling my way around a world and learning its shape and contours. Who are these people? Who do they know? Where are we? What's going on? It's where I start thinking and knowing what I'm doing; the second draft is where I really live with the knowledge; the third draft is where I figure out what the book is about; and the fourth draft is where I'm trying to make it as good as possible.

SM: Do you enjoy this process?

KS: I always start a first draft thinking, 'Oh, this time it's all in the first draft', but it never is. With *Home Fire* (Bloomsbury, 2017), it was to a greater extent because the novel is based on a 2,000-year-old play (*Antigone*) and much of the storyline and the characters I was working with were already there. That was a novel that was mainly done by the second draft. As a result, I enjoyed it less than I enjoyed writing anything else, because for me the fun comes in the third and fourth draft. I am very comfortable with the idea of having to do massive work to rewrite, with throwing out a central character, with deleting 30,000 words—it doesn't bother me. The only thing that matters is getting the book to be the best it can be.

SM: And with these early drafts is your editor your first reader?

KS: The first draft will very often go just to my agent, who is a very good reader and editor—not all agents are. Sometimes she'll return the draft to me, and other times, she'll send it straight on to my editors—one in America and the other in the UK. I have a couple of friends whom I also show early drafts to—they're both writers and one of them did her MFA with me long ago in Massachusetts, and has read early drafts of every one of my eight novels. It's really useful to have someone in your life who knows you, knows the kind of thing you're interested in doing, and can also speak straight without feeling the need to sugar-coat things. I think you have to judge wisely who those people are.

SM: What does one look for in a first reader?

KS: You should look for someone who knows writing—that's the crucial thing. A lot of people will go to their best friend or partner or parent, and that's often a bad idea because you don't want to take feedback personally. If someone is very close to you, maybe they're reading you into the book, or maybe you're reading them into their criticisms. You want to find someone you trust as a reader.

Then, when you get responses back—it's very hard to listen to criticism—it's possible to get very angry. I've learned to pay particular attention to moments when I do feel angry over feedback because there are two reasons for anger. One is because I feel the person hasn't been reading closely enough and they've missed something, and if they have, that's on them—they are bad readers. But the other reason I may get angry is because they're right about something that is deeply wrong in my work. If I'm angry for that reason, I need to really stop and think.

I teach creative writing and I never let the person whose work is being discussed speak while everyone talks. You don't need to justify your work; either you are confident in the work you've done, or there's something that needs to be fixed. It's very useful to go away after listening to criticism and just sit with it for a while, and see after a day or two how you feel about it.

SM: Do you have the same approach to reviews? I'm terrified to read reviews; I don't want to read any reviews and I know a lot of people who don't. Do you?

KS: I read all my reviews.

SM: How do you walk away from a review that isn't great?

KS: There are always going to be reviews that aren't great. It's also what we mean by 'great'. There are some reviews that are full of praise, and yet, to me, are irritating because they are getting it wrong and reading into the book something they want to see, and that can actually be more irritating than a review that is critical but smart. I have learned a thing or two from reviews that don't like something in the work. Obviously, it stings when they're right, but I say, 'Well, okay, I can respect that.'

My day has never been made or ruined by a review; my hour has been, but not my day. I suppose, by the time a book is out in the world, I know it, and I also, now, know that reviewers get things right and wrong all the time. Sometimes you're lucky about which reviewer is paired with your book and sometimes you're not. But the other thing is that a lot of the books that I love the most are really messy books that one can find all kinds of faults with.

SM: Can you give an example?

KS: *Seven Moons of Maali Almeida* by Shehan Karunatilaka, and Shehan's first novel, *Chinaman*. You could, if you wanted to find fault with Shehan's books, say, 'There's too much dialogue, there are too many people, there's so much going on, everything is spilling out.' With both his books, when I started reading, that was my feeling, but there's also enough there, always, that is wonderful and that pulls me along, and then, at a certain point, I see it's really working. It's this big, rambunctious, generous, crazy thing. A lot of my books are also often messy; there is a lot going on. It's not a neat clean line that goes from beginning to end. I know there will be readers that won't like that.

SM: *Home Fire* won the 2018 Women's Prize and was hugely successful. Did you feel any pressure while writing *Best of Friends*?

KS: I'm very grateful I didn't have that kind of success early on. I would hope for all the people who are working on their first novel that it does well in the world, but I think it would be very destabilizing to have a huge success right away. I know people it's happened to and it's terrible, because it doesn't give you enough sense of what a normal publishing experience is.

My first book (*In the City by the Sea*, Granta, 1998) got some nice reviews, but it didn't sell a lot of copies and I wasn't invited to literary festivals. But the first round of nice reviews really did matter. It was exciting to walk into bookshops to see it there, and the fact that I had a novel that was published, that someone was actually giving me money for—it wasn't a lot of money—that in itself was thrilling enough.

I was very lucky to have *Home Fire* do as well as it's done, and it's very possible no novel I will write will do that again. But what *Home Fire* did was that it ensured that the novel after it had a huge boost of publicity. I'm grateful for that, and I also know that I won't always enjoy this level of success. It's part of the game. Once you get into the process of writing, you just shut out everything else, and it just becomes about the difficulties and challenges of doing the writing itself.

SM: Is *Home Fire*, and the themes it addresses, something you would have written a few years ago?

KS: I wouldn't have written *Home Fire* before I became a British citizen—I'm very clear about that. I couldn't have thought of writing a book that was as deeply and profoundly critical of the British government. Was that because I hadn't lived in Britain long enough? I moved to London in 2007 and became a citizen in 2013. I was working on *Burnt Shadows* (Picador, 2009), which I had started when I was still living in Karachi, and *A God in Every Stone* (Bloomsbury, 2014) which, I suppose, is critical of Empire, but it's a slightly different thing to be taking on the actual laws of the time.

There are always these internal dialogues about what we feel free to write about, or don't, that we aren't always strictly aware of. I remember years ago being on a panel with a group from Singapore, and being asked a question about censorship. There were five writers, I think, and four of them said, we write whatever we want to, and then the fifth said, 'Yes, you see, that has been the success of the Singapore government. They have placed these internal censors so deep inside us, we don't see them.' I'm sure there are things about Pakistan I wouldn't write about.

SM: Do you write your first draft in a linear way for the story to progress?

KS: I always write in absolute linear fashion: Page One, Page Two, Page Three; Chapter One, Chapter Two, Chapter Three.

It's because, as I said before, the writing engenders the writing, so this sentence will influence a sentence that comes after, and so on—I don't know how to write in any other way. Sometimes I come across writers who say, 'Oh, there are certain bits that we know are fun and exciting and we just write those first.' I say, 'No, you have to think of it in this way: Do you want to always have those rewards first?'

There are certain kinds of scenes that we do better and that are more fun for us. But if we write all of those first, then what we're left with is this, 'Oh now I've got the not-fun-stuff, or the stuff that's harder', and that can feel quite daunting. There's a lot to be said for writing the difficult bits, and boring bits, with the easy bits.

SM: I am curious about what you are excited to read from this part of the world.

KS: It's not so much about subject matter, but the way a book's written. I've been on a very good run of reading. So there's Shehan's *The Seven Moons of Maali Almeida*, which is about Sri Lanka and the messiness of the aftermath of war and extrajudicial killings; Claire Keegan's *Small Things like These*, which is the opposite—a really slim, taut novel about a man in Ireland and certain things that are going on in the convent up the road that he's supposed to ignore; Andrew Greer's *Less*, which is a romantic comedy about a writer on the road, pining for and trying to pretend he's not pining for the person he loved; Yiyun Li's *The Book of Goose*, which is another novel of friendship, about two teenagers in France, and one of them writes a novel and they publish it under the other one's name; and Stephen Buoro's *The Five Sorrowful Mysteries of Andy Africa*, which is set in Nigeria. I'm not going to these because of subject matter; often it comes down to opening and reading the first page, and something pulls me in.

SM: Can you tell us what your writing routine is like?

KS: When I'm starting off, my writing process is very sporadic. Then I get sick of myself and write five days a week. I wake up in the morning, have a cup of tea or coffee, read the newspapers, and then sit at my desk. How long I stay at my desk can vary, but it's usually about four or five hours, and if I do decent work, that's a day's writing. When I'm later in the process, and I get to the point where I'm becoming a bit obsessive about it, then I sit much longer, and often have to force myself to pull away, because I realize that my brain is turning to mush, and the sentences are coming out badly. Five days a week, first thing in the morning. When I was working on *A God in Every Stone*, 200 words in a day felt like a good day's work, but with most novels it's 400 a day, which doesn't sound like a lot, but is actually all you need. But there are days when I get stuck, and it's very useful to get up and go for a walk. I'm not too strict with myself about how long I stay at the desk, it's more the start time that I try to be consistent about.

SM: We have been discussing *Home Fire* and *A God in Every Stone* and your earlier books. What do you think of them now?

KS: I feel the sort of affection that I feel for my younger self. I made some mistakes, there were things I didn't know, but I had the energy of youth. I stand by every one of them. There's no book of mine that if you hand me a copy and say, 'I really love this', I'd grimace. I'm delighted when people pick up the ones that are less talked about. Of all my novels the one that I love the most is *A God in Every Stone*. I could probably read it again.

SM: Why that book?

KS: It appeals to the nerdy parts of me. There's a lot of my particular nerdy interests from archaeology to early twentieth century politics.

SM: How do you balance instinctive writing with research, and writing after research, if you need to do both?

KS: There have been a couple of my books, *Burnt Shadows* and *A God in Every Stone*, where I've had to do huge amounts of research, and I do have that nerdy side where, if I'm interested in something, I go deep. I research to the point where I feel I have enough knowledge and information to get going. But, as I'm proceeding, I carry on researching and the first draft will usually have too much research, because there are all these interesting things I found out that I want to throw in. In the revisions, I go back and think, 'I don't really need to be showing off about all the things I know.'

SM: And how do you know when an idea is good and how do you stick with it?

KS: The way it works for me is that I'll finish a novel and feel just depleted, and then a certain amount of time goes by and I feel my brain rattling around in my head thinking, 'What am I doing?' Then, it's almost like this antenna goes up and I'm scanning. I'm just looking for what is interesting, and sometimes an idea or an image will strike me. I just sit and wait to see if that idea sticks around, and sometimes it does, and other ideas or images start to attach themselves to it—like this gravitational force pulling ideas, images, characters—and when enough of those are spinning around, I think, 'Okay, this really does want to become a novel.'

SM: Have you ever had to shelve an idea because you felt it was very good but perhaps there wasn't a lot of interest in it? What do you do if that's the case?

KS: No, because that would mean shelving a book, because I never show anyone anything I've done until I finish the first draft. It's not that the idea would be shared. There are some people who will sit and talk to editors or other people about their ideas, and have a conversation about if this is interesting or not; I've never done that. I just sit and write a draft, and then I send it on.

SM: Do you have advice for people who are working on something they care about but haven't received the interest that they hoped for?

KS: Publishing is hard and I sit at the privileged end of it, all these years later. It's hard to get that initial interest, I think, much more than was the case when I first started. Agents want you to be your own marketing department and to find a way to write in one sentence the elevator pitch that is going to strike them as, 'Here's this wonderful idea that the world can't do without.'

No piece of writing is ever wasted. If you believe in a project, and it's the thing you want to write, work those writing muscles, learn what you can, but don't obsess about it. Finish one, do your best for it, send it out to the world, and if you get rejections it's to do with the fact that publishing is a business where marketing departments have increasing amounts of power, and sometimes they don't have the imagination to know how to read certain kinds of books, or how to sell them.

I remember with one of my earliest books, *Salt and Saffron*, the American publisher was not very keen and kind of just took it on—I don't know why—paid very little money and got it. When I was in New York, the publicity person said, 'Well, you're going to have to help me out here because I don't know how to reach your community.' It was only after I left the room that I thought I should have answered, 'Readers.' But, of course, you don't say that.

So, there are those kinds of responses, particularly if you are writing in a space that is different to the one you're writing about and grew up in. The truth of publishing is that there are quite fixed expectations, particularly with newer writers, of what writing from certain parts of the world should look like.

SM: And one last question. What do you love most about this job?

KS: I deeply love the late revision stage, where I know the world I'm writing about and I know what I'm doing. It's just pure pleasure for me. The last draft is when I'm having fun and I'm in the zone. It's also incredibly lovely to be able to earn a living doing what I have always wanted to do.

MANJUSHREE THAPA

INTERVIEWED BY

ROMAN GAUTAM

~

'Fight for your right to be a complex human being'

Roman Gautam (RG): For me, growing up in Kathmandu in the 1990s, there weren't many books, especially for a young adult, to learn about what was happening in the country. This was, of course, a period of great turmoil, with the civil war. You wrote a book called *Forget Kathmandu* (Penguin, 2005), which is still a touchstone for so many people trying to understand what was happening in Nepal through the 1990s and into the early 2000s, and I think it speaks a lot to what you do and your stature and importance. Of course, it's not the only book of yours that everyone keeps going to; *The Tutor of History* (Penguin, 2001), your first novel, was a bestseller, and with good reason. For me, what's been most meaningful about reading your works is that there's always a real glimpse of Nepal. You helped me understand what was happening in my country when I was younger, and you've been doing that for so many other people. You have probably reached more readers in the Anglophone world than any Nepali writer today. How did you chart your early course? And how do you understand your balance now, as a writer between the real and fictional worlds?

Manjushree Thapa (MT): I'm going to start by talking about ancient history, which is: before you're a writer, you're a reader. The people who were influencing me as I was forming as a human being—not even as a writer—were people who wrote about the peripheries, travel writers like Bruce Chatwin and Paul Theroux, who wrote in English. There was this entire genre of travel writing, and I was growing up reading it, even though, unbeknownst to me as a young person, that genre was dying out because of Edward Said's *Orientalism* and the political problem of writers from the centre—from places of power—studying 'the Other' and writing about them.

That was dying out, and yet it was the only really accessible way into writing about the peripheries for someone like me who was writing in English, was not just from South Asia, but from Nepal, which was even more in the periphery than, let's say, India. I was looking at writers of the generation just above me; Salman Rushdie's book about Nicaragua, *The Jaguar Smile*; Amitav Ghosh's *Dancing in Cambodia, at Large in Burma* and books by Vikram Seth. These were the models that were available to me as a Nepali writer writing in English, wanting to write about this tiny little corner I really cared about, so I think I started my career with travel writing. That was how I broke into writing.

Very soon after, I wrote *Mustang Bhot in Fragments* (1992), which is about a remote part of Nepal on the Tibet border. I am from the centre of Nepal, Kathmandu, and going to the periphery within the periphery and writing about the Other made me very uncomfortable. After that, I switched to non-fiction that was, nevertheless, personal. The influence of writers like Ryszard Kapuściński, or Rian Malan—who writes about the complicity of the elite South Africans in Apartheid—was formative for me. These kinds of personal voices in non-fiction were what I veered towards in travel writing.

RG: And in terms of your path through both fiction and non-fiction from there on, how have you seen your juggling act, if we can call it that, and how do you think both have shaped your way and charted your course?

MT: I was in my late twenties at that point, and I felt stuck on the outside of my subjects. I wanted to write with an interior voice—to get inside my human subjects—and write from the inside. I've always been interested in the politics and the social issues of our time, and I wanted to be a contemporary writer writing about these issues. But I decided that I need to not just write fiction, but master the craft—it was a decision I made when I was twenty-six or twenty-seven years old.

I woke up one morning and said, 'I just have to get my head around the craft of fiction.' So, I attended one of those American MFA programmes—which are very famous now for sometimes being of great use and sometimes of not being of much use. I was lucky because I got to use those two years to really immerse myself in honing my writing skills. I already had the material that I wanted to write about and I had my themes. I also had my basic creative impulse, which is a documentary impulse, and I wanted to respond to my world and the times I was living through in Nepal, but in a way that reflected the real world. I wanted to have a realist aesthetic, but I needed to plunge into the craft.

I took two years out and just experimented and experimented before I wrote my first novel, *The Tutor of History*. I was working on short stories—an easier space for experimentation—and I tried everything because, for me, I realized that my creative mother was Virginia Woolf. I wanted to write fiction with interiority.

There were other writers who were very influential for me—Don DeLillo, who writes about the madness of American society but with a very particular voice, and Teresa Hak Kyung Cha, who wrote *Dictee*, a very political, social, historical document but with a beautiful poetic voice. I knew that was what I was aiming for. The short stories in *Tilled Earth* (Penguin, 2007), which came out after my novel, are stories that I wrote over a period of about ten years that document my journey, my search for aesthetics. I knew what my ethics were as a writer, but I didn't have a style, a voice and a craft to match. *Tilled Earth* traces my growth, and I can look at it now and see that some stories are very conservative or conventionally written, and some are really 'blasted open' and experimental. That was what I was trying to move towards, but I actually arrived at it later.

RG: *The Tutor of History* was set in a very recognizable time and place for anyone from Nepal, during a decade of democracy and democratic experimentation in the 1990s. You had an ensemble cast and a lot of the nitty-gritty on how Nepali society and Nepali democratic elections were configured. I want to ask you about form. What models of the novel did you consider before you settled on a suitable vessel for what you were trying to say?

MT: I wrote that novel, my first, as my MFA thesis. I did a lot of soul searching and a lot of searching for craft in between, and in the main, I arrived at two or three things. One is Mikhail Bakhtin's thought that novels, in particular, are dialogical—you don't have the one logic; you have many different logics running through them. Because I was writing about a democratic moment in Nepal, when suddenly everything opened up and we were all equal citizens for the first time in my lifetime, I wanted to have more than one protagonist—so I had four main protagonists. I decided I wanted to have a big social canvas, so there were secondary characters, and also tertiary, and there's the community as a whole. So, it ended up being a novel, that while I was learning the ropes of how to write fiction, kind of got away from me.

For me, looking back at that novel, I'm really glad I did that, because that's what I wanted to do, but it was a five-year struggle with the material. The novel has flashes of the later voice that I arrived at as a writer, but mostly it's a first novel where you see the writer grappling with material that's a little bit out of her control—I read it that way now. I'm glad I went through that process, because that period of looking for craft and struggling was crucial. There were many times when I thought the novel would never be done; I thought I had just sunk myself into my first book and I would never get out of it.

RG: I wanted to ask you to talk about making that daunting leap, which you made with your second book. Can you cast your mind back to the questions you were asking yourself then, and the answers you were finding?

MT: I think a lot of writers arrive at their work through very different means. For me, the theoretical and the political were always really important, and I came at novel-writing backwards. Once I clarified my theme, which is contemporary Nepali life and particularly the struggle between societal constraints and individual freedom—that's roughly what all of my work has hovered around—then I looked for craft that served that.

We've talked about my second book, which was a big social novel, then the book after that is *Forget Kathmandu*, which again is non-fiction with a personal voice. I was shifting back and forth in terms of genre, but I wanted to write about contemporary Nepal and the search for freedom and liberty, and what that meant in the middle of everything Nepal had been through—the royalist coup, Maoist insurgencies. That was the line that I could draw through all of my work. The one thing young writers should fight for—and I hope it's possible—is to move between genres, because publishing houses tend to be quite nervous about introducing a writer and then having them stray from what their marketability might be.

I was really lucky I had an editor who I met with my first novel, Ravi Singh, with Speaking Tiger now, who was at Penguin India then. I gave him the novel and we started our collaboration. The relationship with an editor is important and he and I often think of our collaboration as 'growing up together', because he was starting out as an editor and I was starting out as a writer. I trusted him when he gave feedback, and he trusted—while I was skipping around fiction to non-fiction—that what I was writing was going to work. That was possibly the most important working relationship I had. In the West you need agents, and those are important professional relationships, but in South Asia, from what I know so far, you may not require an agent. The creative relationship with the editor is absolutely central, and certainly was central in terms of me moving forward as a writer. I don't think I answered your question, Roman.

RG: My question was really just a prompt to get you to talk about the questions you were asking and the realizations you were coming to through that process of making that big leap, and I think you're very much answering that.

MT: I'll talk about the ethics. I was living in Nepal during this entire time and my peers and elders were divided into two factions—by which I mean Nepali-language writing was divided into two factions. One was the democratic flank, and I would say someone like Mohan Koirala, who wrote experimental poetry, exemplified that, and then there was the progressive flank, mostly communist writers, who adopted social realist aesthetics and were very much marked by Chinese and Soviet literature. For me, it was really productive, creatively, to be reading my elders and peers in the Nepali language even though I was writing in English, because that gave me a sense of the intellectual milieu I was coming out of, and the intellectual milieu that my characters or their nation were inhabiting. Beginning to translate these writers became absolutely central as a way to resolve issues in my own writing.

Even though I identified more with the progressive flank of Nepali literature, there was a very big barrier for me between the socialist realist writing that my peers were producing and my own ideas. Their writing was stamped by communist aesthetics; they could be quite utilitarian in how they portrayed their characters—the good guys and the bad guys, the exploiters and the exploited. These were novels of revolution. I admired the effort and recognized the genre, but I had studied in the United States, where the Frankfurt School of the post-Fascist left had really imprinted itself on me in terms of an ethical response to the world. I could not really emulate my communist peers in Nepal. I wondered, as a Nepali writer, where do I stand in this milieu, where do I belong in all of this?

I tried for a while to write in both languages—my Nepali is a lot worse than my English because of how I was educated and raised—but then I decided that the best use of my skills was to translate the work of Nepali writers I admire. That not just made me useful in the Nepali literary world, but also changed my own writing, because I learned how to write in English about my subjects who live in a Nepali-language world, who inhabit another language in their inner lives. I learned how to write about their worlds in English through the art of translation.

RG: I do want to say here that you've produced multiple works of translation, including of some classics of Nepali writing. For example, the late Indra Bahadur Rai's *Aaja Ramita Chha* (*There's a Carnival Today*), a great book and probably one of the most popular books in the Nepali language that you brought into English in a beautiful way. Building on what you were saying about translation, and combined with the politics that you were mentioning earlier of the centre and the periphery, I want to ask how you've charted a course through that politics in your writing and in the translations you've worked on. What do you think of those politics now, on this side of your journey?

MT: There's been a splintering of our understanding of what is the centre and what is the periphery. This is particularly so, right now, with translation being the hot trend in publishing—it's not big enough still, but it's getting more attention than it ever has. When I was a young writer, I had a very clear sense of the globe and the periphery, and there was a centre—or I imagined that there was one. Now that has, of course, splintered. If you're a Nepali writer from Kathmandu, as I am, then you are already the centre, part of what many people in Nepal call a 'colonial power' over other communities in Nepal. So, there's been a splintering along civil rights issues. Nepal has 120 or more languages and there's the hegemony of the Nepali language, not to mention the power of the English language—all of this has been questioned.

It's a challenge because people who are very comfortable—and here I'll take as an example the leftist flank of Nepali writing from my generation—positioning themselves as speaking for those who cannot speak have now been challenged, saying, 'But you're from the upper caste', 'You're from an elite community'. People are now able to speak for themselves in their own languages, with their own complexities. It's absolutely important to pay attention to that and make space for that.

I think it's a time of tumult, in some way, in the Nepali intellectual world, which is also fragmented along diasporic lines. For me, the move out of Kathmandu to Toronto, where I've been for about ten years, was creatively very confusing, because I always wrote in the middle of the environment that I was writing about, and there was always inspiration in the air. Writing from a distance has been very confusing for me. I've still not got my head around it.

I also think I needed a break from the intensity of living in Kathmandu, where almost every day there was a crisis. If you're a creative person, you're trying to respond to the contemporary moment, and it becomes overwhelming. Right now, I'm in a period where I am trying to get my head around the distance. As for diasporic writing, I will say that there's an earlier generation of writers who almost wrote more about their parents' generation— about their lives as immigrants. I'll take Jhumpa Lahiri, who writes about an immigrant family, as an example. I think that is much less interesting for my generation who inhabit both worlds. You can go to Jackson Heights and have exactly the same conversation you're having in a tea shop in Kathmandu, right? I find this sort of simultaneity of identity, this mixed-in-ness, the mongrel-ization of all of these cultures, more creatively interesting.

RG: For young writers who are grappling with the same things, what would you recommend in terms of maintaining connections, which I think are so vital for anybody's creativity.

MT: For me, fighting for the right to be a complex human being, to be a contradictory, mixed-in, mongrelized person with conflicting loyalties, is really important. This flies against the traditions of publishing, which will want to pigeonhole you as, 'Oh, this is a writer from Nepal', and give you a narrow range of what to write about. It's a real pressure for many people who want to make a living as writers. The publishing industry has its conventions for a reason; that is how writers are more marketable. It's been important for me to step back and say, 'Look, I need to keep evolving as a writer, and I need to be honest to my writing desires. I don't want to be just a writer from Nepal who did this in the past. I'm going to write in the future.'

I'm working on a novel now, I want to work on translations, and I have at least two non-fiction books that I really want to write. If I'm going to work on those, I'm going to have to fight for that space. There is no such thing as an established literary career anymore. I've written ten books and every book is a creative struggle, every book is a bit of a struggle to convince my publisher to publish. That is just part of the challenge of being a writer, I'm afraid. I don't want to discourage anyone, but I do think that we get one shot at this, right? So, if you find yourself writing things that you've been steered into, that are not deeply satisfying, then just fight for yourself, absolutely.

RG: You're juggling things that so many people trade in exclusively. I mean, they would treat fiction, non-fiction and translation as three different things to do, and try to only specialize in one. In today's context, it's almost surprising to find somebody who's doing all three, and what you're talking about in terms of using those as tools to stay engaged with the things that feed you, feed your heart and feed your creative mind, I think, is huge. You were talking earlier about your creative relationship with your editor, and I wanted to ask you to talk more about that. As an editor, I've seen the power and importance of that relationship, but I also know that for people on the outside it's very difficult to appreciate and understand. Perhaps you could shine some light on it.

MT: It's really important to look for editors who have published the kind of work that you write. It's very easy to be mismatched with editors because there are many good editors who are not interested in the kind of work you're doing. I was just lucky that I fell into a writer–editor relationship with someone with complete understanding and also space to grow with. As a writer I've always looked to editors to show me things I'm not seeing in my own work, including possibilities and potential I had not realized, and also, sometimes, things I was totally unaware I was doing in terms of the finer skills—reliance on certain sentence structures or craft points. An editor can say, 'Look, this is what you're doing. Did you mean to do this intentionally?' Or, 'Cut this out. This is not good.'

In the West these days, agents often play the role of quasi-editors, where they do the first read and give you a sense of where you could move the book, if they think it's more marketable one way, or better the other. When I was forming as a writer, I had a circle of writers and we shared work with each other. That was really important. It was gentle, but supportive and helpful.

When I was beginning to translate and to read about translation, Gayatri Chakravorty Spivak was extremely influential, intellectually, ethically, and also aesthetically. As a translator she's amazing. I wanted to also talk about fiction and non-fiction— the kind of range some editors will allow, and others will be less enthusiastic about. As I moved forward in terms of non-fiction— having begun with travel writing, then a journalistic, personal essayist kind of writing, and later, towards creative non-fiction—all of that got nurtured because I was allowed something like a 10–12 year period where I could write anything, and my excellent editor, Ravi Singh, would respond very constructively to it.

RG: You were talking about how that space for experimentation that was afforded to you was not afforded to many writers, or not as frequently afforded to writers nowadays. I'm curious to hear why that's the case. What are the forces that a young writer will need to fight against?

MT: When I began to publish, I was publishing in South Asia, primarily. It has been a very rapidly expanding field of publishing. Penguin India had just started up and David Davidar had just established himself as an editor. Then, a lot of people he worked with ended up heading the other private publishing houses that came up subsequently, and that trend is continuing. There are more and more publishing houses and spaces, including online ones, opening up. There's more pressure to establish writers early on, and if the first book isn't successful, it's harder and harder to give a writer a chance to publish a second or third book. This is particularly true in the West, where it's very ruthless right now, and if your second book doesn't do well, it's very hard to get the next contract.

RG: You talked about the difficulty of writing about Nepal while living in Canada, but does distance from one's subject offer any advantages at all?

MT: I've yet to find the advantages. I've read interviews of writers who have said that they found it helpful to have distance from their subjects. For me, I'm still in the middle of a transition, creatively, from writing about Nepal from Nepal, to writing about it from afar. There's a distillation of what matters. I'm now in my fifties, I'm working on my umpteenth book, and it's still a creative problem for me because of the distance. I only see disadvantages to it, which is why I spend a lot of time in Nepal. I know other writers have found advantages, so maybe it's just me, or maybe it's because I was formed as a writer in situ, in Nepal, not as a diaspora writer.

RG: What was the process like for you to connect with your Nepali roots through translation?

MT: When I decided to start writing fiction is when I took it seriously and that's when I also started reading Nepali literature. Nepali literature is relatively young for South Asian literature— it's a 100–150-years-old modern literature, so I really made it a project to work through the classics. Then I began to notice the overwhelming dominance of high caste, male writers, and started to search out other writers in other languages, women writers, writers from other communities. I began to translate them and that to me was absolutely crucial, because otherwise the space for English writing in Nepal was exclusive. I remember the early term for writers like us were 'writers from India writing in English' or 'from South Asia writing in English', and I agree that that group tended to come from the so-called 'creamy layer'—the term used in a denigrating way. I was one of the early generation to study in English schools in Nepal. But now there are entire crops of people from very diverse backgrounds who have studied and who write in English, so it's less true now that Nepal's English writing is from the creamy layer.

It was absolutely grounding for me to understand that I was, as an English writer, not writing in a void—I had all of these peers in Nepal's 120-plus languages. There was this big literary dialogue going on, and Nepal, like any place in Asia, has a hectic literary scene. There are a lot of books coming out, a lot of book reviews, a lot of dialogue around books. It was very humbling, it was grounding and it certainly made me realize that writing in English doesn't make you a better writer; often, it makes you a worse writer about your country or society.

Something I'd recommend to any writer, whatever other languages are available to you, is to read in those, and if you can translate as a creative practice, I would recommend that as well. One of the more enriching ways to learn how to write in English is by translating, let's say, a Nepali text into English. You learn how to write with the complexity that the Nepali language affords, but in English. That is a technical problem that we all have to resolve in our English writing, and that is solved by learning how to translate. My engagement with the reading of Nepali literature, and the translating, has been formative for me.

RG: I'm interested to know your thoughts on first drafts, especially for novels. How do we push forward through to the finish line? Over time, the story seems to expand. When does research stop for you?

MT: Research is so much fun. I love research. It's when you put it down into the first draft that the fun ends. Everyone has a different process, but for me, the first draft is like pulling teeth. It is horrendous. I cringe with every sentence I write. But the goal is to put everything down—whether it's the plot or even just markers for the plot. If I cannot write a scene where something happens, I say, 'Okay, this scene goes here', and I start with an outline and then flesh it out. I revise a lot and after the third or fourth draft, the magic begins where the sentences and the craft come together to bring the story to life.

In my experience, the research has to stop at some point, and then, while you're writing, you will know that this section needs more research and you can go back and research things for a later draft. It's important to get through the first draft and put it all down. You have to recognize 'What's enough research?' and if it is an excuse for avoiding writing the book. You have to grit your teeth and get through it—that's how I do it. Then you can either go back and research more, or cut out the research that you've done if it's too much. Roman, as an editor, would you second that?

RG: Yes, the most important thing is just to get it down on paper. But something I'd like to add is that losing track while in the depths of despair when writing the first draft, doesn't change. For me, as an editor, and in my education as an editor, the understanding of that process has been very important. I think writing is rewriting alone, editing is rewriting too, and editing and writing together with an editor means you get to do the whole process with a friend. It's important to keep in mind that you're not under pressure to produce something like Gabriel García Márquez's published work when you sit down at your laptop straight off the bat. Everybody who is part of that process—mentors, friends, editors, agents—will be helping, and you're going to have to keep asking, 'How do I make this better and better and better?' So, just take that pressure off of yourself. You're not going to write genius prose and plot from day one. If you've got talent, I think it will come, and you should have faith in that talent but also just embrace the pain.

MT: I also want to say that before you start a first draft, draw an outline, particularly for long pieces. Have the architecture, the overall structure of the piece you want, before you write the story down. You want to make sure you're not following any dead ends. Outlining is absolutely the first step, then the first draft, and then as many drafts as it takes. My first novel took me five years and possibly something above twenty-five drafts. I just kept going back and refining this or that. Yes, writing is rewriting.

MANSI CHOKSI

INTERVIEWED BY

SANAM MAHER

❧

'I love the private torture of writing'

Sanam Maher (SM): *The Newlyweds* (Simon & Schuster, 2022) is one of the best things I've read. I am so impressed with the way you told the story and how you deal with love and marriage, tradition and modernity, disappointment and identity through a very intimate look at the lives of three couples in India. Can you tell me how the idea came to you?

Mansi Choksi (MC): I wanted to write about the Love Commandos, which is a charity that promises to protect young lovers who have been marked for honour killings by their families. The organization was featured in an episode of *Satyamev Jayate*, and when I saw it, I thought, 'I'm going to go to Delhi and write a piece that says something about these wonderful middle-aged men that are putting their lives at great risk to protect young lovers.' I pitched the story for several years, but everyone said no. Then I got a fellowship to go to Sri Lanka for a separate story, and thought, 'Maybe I'll just go from Sri Lanka to Delhi at my own cost, spend some time with the Love Commandos, and write a more robust pitch.' That was the first time I met Sanjoy Sachdev, who runs the group. The first day I went there, I was like, 'Okay, this is fantastic. I'm going to write a great piece.' I went back every day for a week at which point I was able to see the shelter take its natural form. And what it revealed was a man who was accused of preying on vulnerable people who had come to him for help.

I pitched the story to *Harper's Magazine*,[3] wrote the article, and that was the beginning.

After *Harper's*, I knew I wanted to create a piece of work about the lives of young people who were born in villages and small cities, and had grown up at a time of great economic growth and optimism. I wanted to spend more time in the aftermath, when the dramatic power of the great Indian love story had fizzled away. What happens to love after it is attained? Does it become less valuable or does it get replaced with regret and wanting to return to the family structures that one fought against? We often think of love as a subversive force that can bridge divides. One of the couples in my book, Arif and Monika, are a Hindu–Muslim couple that got caught at the centre of a so-called 'love jihad' controversy. By the end of the story, Monika feels burning contempt for the poverty of her husband's family and resents the fact that she is now married to a Muslim.

SM: Your pitch changed after your first visit to the Love Commandos. Did that make you nervous?

MC: It actually made the pitch more interesting. The Love Commandos had by then been written about by hundreds of magazines and newspapers. Every Valentine's Day their story was a staple in India. Someone would do a glowing profile like, 'Oh look at this saviour of young lovers.' I had to be really persistent, and make myself small and unthreatening, so that Sanjoy Sachdev would let me linger. He probably thought, 'What is she going to do?' I didn't even have a publication behind me. It was just me, my

---

3 Mansi Choksi, 'The Newlyweds: What's at Stake When You Marry for Love?', *Harper's Magazine*.

notebook and recorder. I would just keep showing up. I'd be like, 'Oh, I got you some idlis.' The next day I would say, 'I got you samosas.' That was the only way I could keep buying more time.

SM: How clear were you about the themes you wanted to explore?

MC: After this piece did well and agents showed interest, I had to think about what I was going to do for a book-length project. I thought about using a love story to tell a larger story about the big changes happening in India. I wanted to tell the story about a same-sex couple, because Section 377 was being debated at the time. I chose Arif and Monika because their story was a good way to illustrate India's lurch to the right. Another couple's story demonstrated the capitalist nature of modern India.

SM: The way you tell the stories is so intimate. There were so many points in the book where I wondered how you got the level of detail.

MC: Young people record everything. One of the women I profiled, Neetu, told me she liked to keep a diary. So, I bought her a new diary and said, 'You should write an entry every day.' The next time I met her, she had an entry for every day that I had not been there. It was a goldmine of access. With Arif and Monika, a lot of their elopement conversations happened on Facebook. And again I lucked out because they gave me access to their account. I was able to go into their chats and read them as if it were happening in real time.

SM: What about when you were in the field? Can you talk about how you work?

MC: I really changed the way I work after we lost Kim Wall. Kim and I were very good friends from graduate school. We did a bunch of reporting trips together, including the one in Sri Lanka before Love Commandos. She was killed while on assignment, so I think a lot about safety now when I go into the field. Usually, I will try to find a place where there is a middle-aged woman at some near distance from where I am working. I feel it's safest to find an aunty nearby, to run to if something feels wrong. I also tell my husband, my mom, and maybe a friend where I am and in how long to expect me back, because I usually turn off my phone. I let them know that after three hours I'll turn my phone on and send a message saying, 'I'm fine.' And that if they don't hear from me they should send someone to check. When I go into a place, I listen to myself. If I feel unsafe, I just leave. I don't care what's happening to the story.

SM: These are really difficult stories: these couples are away from their families, they've gone through a lot. How did you approach them and make them feel comfortable?

MC: I would let my tape recorder run the whole day. That was probably not the smartest thing to do, because I would come back to hours and hours of tape. But in terms of collecting scenes, this was the main thing that helped. I would also write myself a note at the end of the day about the things that stuck out for me—the smells, a particular dialogue. I gathered photos, videos and court documents. And before I started writing about a person, I would make a 'Top 10' list, featuring ten things about them that had struck me and which I wanted to bring out.

SM: Can you give us an example?

MC: There was this one day that I was hanging out with Monika in the village that she was living in with Arif, when Arif's mother came in to drop off some food. Monika said, 'Her breath smells; it is of an empty stomach.' It was such a raw line and really summed up, for me, what Monika's central conflict was. She was so full of regret for all the things she had given up in order to be with Arif. Another time Monika was trying out a new burkha that her mother-in-law had gifted her, and she said, 'When I go to Bombay, I'm going to drop this and wear whatever I want. Nobody can stop me because I am a girl that was made for a big city.' That summed up the aspirational quality of what Monika thought a love marriage was going to achieve for her. She kept waiting for that time and it never really came.

SM: I love the idea of a 'Top 10', I'm going to steal that, for sure. Did you ever feel daunted by all the material?

MC: I started with a basic map of the book, so I knew there was going to be Part One, Part Two and Part Three. Part One would be from the moment the couples run away, Part Two would have some background about who they were and what made them who they were, and Part Three would be about them reconciling with their actions. That was the broad framework of how the book was distributed and I had a sense of how each of their stories would be cut into those timelines. The writing actually happened at the height of the pandemic. I had a six-month-old baby at the time and no help. I would go downstairs at 5 a.m. and sit there until 11 a.m., and in that time I would aim to produce 200 words.

Then, before bed I would go through those 200 words to make sure they were good words, so that the next day I could start from 201. Of course, there were days where I couldn't follow my routine, but I told myself, 'Take small steps. Don't look at the peak of the mountain, just do your 200 words a day and things will fall into place.'

SM: Did publishers and agents have a set idea of what they wanted a book about India to be about?

MC: None of them wanted another book about India that said something about Narendra Modi. My US publisher, Simon & Schuster, was concerned about whether a random American would pick up the book. Even post publication, I don't think I have an answer to that. As much as I say that love is a universal theme, it's not actually something that draws in a reader that doesn't share the cultural context. I'm now thinking of my second book and really keeping these things in mind. The part for me that I hated the most was the 'post-pub' part. I loved the pitching, I loved the private torture of writing, all of that was fantastic, but when the book went out into the world I experienced a special kind of cruelty that nobody had prepared me for.

I had a really naive understanding of what it means to have a book published. I was like, 'Oh, I'm going to write the best book I can, that I'm proud of, and everything is going to be great.' No, I needed machinery to push my book and make sure that it landed in the hands of the right people at the right time. My publicist was dealing with thirty titles a day, I don't think he cared about pushing this one book from India. The real shocker for me was that I did not get a review in *The New York Times*. After that, nothing made me feel good enough. My book could have been reviewed anywhere and I would have still felt like a massive failure because I was so fixated on *The New York Times*.

SM: Why *The New York Times?*

MC: In early conversations with my editor we talked about what success would look like for the book, and it was clear that success would come from literary acclaim. *The Times* is considered the marquee review publication. Everyone on the team was waiting with bated breath on publication day saying, 'Is the review out, is the review out?' At the end of the day, I got an email from my publicist saying, 'Unfortunately, it doesn't look like there will be a review, because they usually do it on pub day.' It's irrational to equate the success of a book with one review, but publishing a book is like birthing a child and the period after is like postpartum anxiety where you think, 'What is going to happen to this? Is it getting what it needs?' After *The Times* review didn't come out, I went into sixth gear and emailed every book influencer with two followers saying, 'Can you please feature this?' It was a humiliating, dehumanizing experience.

SM: It's a test of endurance. Did it take you time to get back to writing?

MC: I didn't write a good word for about four to five months after the book came out because I became a different version of myself, the book marketing version that is not actually the writer. It was a really emotionally volatile phase and I couldn't work because I was trying to see who would review me, who would do an Insta post, which year-end list I would make. It took away the joy of the whole project, honestly.

SM: How do you look at it now, the book and all the work you put into it?

MC: If I were to do this again, I would toughen myself up, and have my own internal guard rail for what to expect out of the book. It's because I didn't know what to expect, that I subliminally expected everything to happen, and everything that did not happen felt like a disappointment. When I went to New York for the book launch, I met my agent who said, 'This is one of many books that you're going to make. This is one book and it didn't go the way that you wanted it to go, but maybe there's something wrong with the way you wanted it to go.'

SM: I want to end on a question about the couples in the book. What do you feel you owed them?

MC: What I owed them was a super thorough fact check. I annotated the entire manuscript and read each word to the six of them. If they said, 'I was not wearing yellow, I was wearing orange', I'd go with what they said. My aim was to make sure that I was presenting each of them authentically from the point of view of their own truth, because what Monika thinks about Arif's mother may not be *the* truth, but it's *her* truth. That's what I told myself. Now they have turned into friends; I talk to them very, very often. I'm talking to a film producer who's interested in the book and the first people that I shared the news with were the couples. It's exciting for them to imagine themselves as the actors in their own Hindi movie, for their stories to turn into immortal stories.

VAUHINI VARA

INTERVIEWED BY

SAMANTH SUBRAMANIAN

'Stay true to your vision'

Samanth Subramanian (SS): For the few people who might not know who Vauhini Vara is, she is everything. In fact, everything we want to do in our South Asia Speaks programme, every genre of literary writing we aim to target, work on, and write. She does all of those things from both sides of the divide, as a writer and editor—she has worn all the hats we aspire to wear. Most recently, she is a novelist, the author of *The Immortal King Rao*. Congratulations, it's a great book.

Vauhini Vara (VV): Oh, thank you.

SS: I wanted to start by asking you what was the first thing you remember writing?

VV: The very first thing I ever wrote that I remember was in middle school. We had an assignment to write a short story and I'd just watched the kid's movie *The Land Before Time*, which is about cartoon dinosaurs, so I wrote some fan fiction about the dinosaurs. I do remember that my teacher gave me an A+ and said it was great. I remember feeling buoyed by that, and thinking that maybe I could be a writer. That's the first moment I remember actually writing something. I do remember wanting to be a writer pretty young, like around middle school and sort of pursuing it from there, but not in any significant way until I was older.

SS: What did 'pursuing being a writer' look like back in the day? Like in high school through university?

VV: In high school, where I lived—I grew up in Seattle in the 1990s—newspapers were still in existence and successful; this was before the internet. *The Seattle Times* had a summer programme for student journalists of colour. They put us in dorms and taught us journalism, and then we made a newspaper at the end of the two-week programme. The woman who ran that programme also ran a youth newspaper that was tied to *The Seattle Times*, that got sent to all of the high schools in the area. I got a job as her assistant. It was a minimum wage job that paid $7 an hour or something like that, to just work as an assistant in the office of this newspaper for teenagers. That was my first introduction to journalism. At the same time, I would write stories, I would make things up in my diary—I guess that counts as a story—but I didn't really know how to write fiction as such.

Then I went to Stanford, which has a really great creative writing programme. In my second year, I started taking creative writing classes and loved the first class I took. I was encouraged by my professor and met a lot of really close friends including the novelist and South Asia Speaks' mentor, Karan Mahajan. He was one of my first writer friends. We were just kids taking creative writing classes together and I ended up minoring in creative writing. I spent a lot of my time working at the school newspaper, and then a lot of my time taking creative writing classes. That was when I started writing short stories, and when I graduated, I ended up pursuing both at the same time.

SS: You wrote for *The Wall Street Journal* and started an entire blog subsection on *The New Yorker*'s website and you wrote for that as well. Both of these involved relatively shorter forms of writing compared to the much longer magazine pieces you've done. I wanted to ask about when you transition from the shorter to the longer in non-fiction journalism, what are the things you have to think about differently?

VV: There's a lot that changes. I learned it gradually because when I was at *The Wall Street Journal*, I started writing stories that were 2,000 or 2,500 words-long, so I started exercising those muscles. For me, it was a fairly gradual process, moving from that. A front-page story for *The Wall Street Journal* wasn't too different from a magazine story, but there were some skills that I needed to work on. The most useful thing I did when I made the transition was to read a lot. I read *The New Yorker, The Atlantic, The New York Times Magazine* and *Wired*—all the magazines featuring writers I admired. I would take their stories and kind of deconstruct them for myself.

With a couple of my first articles, I thought about similar stories that I'd read and wanted my article or essay to sound like. I would go to the website of that magazine and copy and paste the whole thing into a Google doc, and then I would use comments to figure out for myself how the thing was put together. I would say, 'Okay, the first 500 words are a scene with the main character in this story, and then once you get to about 1,000 words there's a paragraph break, and then there's a long historical section about everything that got us here.' I just studied how it was put together. At first, I would just try to imitate that. I'd be like, 'Okay, well, this works. I'm going to try to do the same thing structurally. My story is a different story, but I want to follow that structure, so my first 500 words are going to be a scene with an important character, but it's going to be the character for my story, and then when I get 1,000 words in, I'm going to have a historical section.'

I don't do that so much anymore, and the reason is that I have that knowledge baked into myself now, from having had practice. But back when I didn't have practice, I just tried to figure out how it was done, and did the same thing. The reason is that the structure of long stories is so different from that for shorter stories, right? You need to sustain an arc, there needs to be something that's keeping a person reading, whether it's some mystery in the plot or a character who's really interesting. Say, at the beginning of the story, there's some question about why they are the way they are, you need to keep reading to find out why. Or, the story takes place somewhere interesting and when you get there, you don't really understand what makes it tick, and you have to keep reading to understand the place. There are all kinds of things, not necessarily a big mystery in every story, but there's always something that's keeping you turning the pages.

I had to figure out how to do that in my way, but what I did early on was to just figure out how others did it, and did the same. There are other ways that you can accomplish that. I also think that as an editor when I'm editing people who are new to this kind of writing, I almost feel that the writing is less of an issue than the reporting or research.

SS: What do you even begin to look for?

VV: For a short piece you might talk to three or four people. Or, for some publications you don't even talk to anybody, right? You just do some reading, write something up and put it together. I think when, and I'm speaking with my editor hat on now, people transition to the longer form, often they don't realize how it's done. You might read a really long thing and be like, 'Well, there are three people quoted in this piece', so maybe they just talked to three people. Or, they're talking about something that happened fifteen years ago, they probably just read a book about it and then wrote about it. But, generally, in this kind of journalism, you try to do first-hand reporting. If you're trying to write about something that happened fifteen years ago, you need to go and find the people involved, and try to talk to them and get their perspectives on what happened. Or, if you're trying to get information about how something works, like a concept or something political, you need to go and talk to all the people involved, and figure out what happened there.

I think what happens when I edit new or emerging writers is, I'll say, 'You say that so and so says that their employer ripped them off and didn't pay them their last paycheque and then disappeared. What did the employer say about this? When you called the boss, what's the boss's version of the story?' And, they might say, 'Oh, I didn't call the boss. The person I'm writing about would get really upset.' But, in journalism, that is something that's required. If you deliberately don't because you're sympathetic towards the employee, the boss could sue you. So, there are all these things that are really important to teach yourself.

SS: One of the things you mentioned was this concept of 'a scene'. The scene to open the article, or the scene that comes midway, and this is important for non-fiction as well as fiction, much more so for fiction, I believe. But, obviously, it's a technique that we borrow from fiction. Can I ask about an example of a scene that you wrote that you thought really worked and why?

VV: You can read articles and say to yourself, 'Oh well, these things all have scenes, and so I guess that's what I need to do. I'll just figure out something that happened in this person's life.' Or, 'When I set out to report the story, something that happened to me, I'll put it in there.' The goal isn't necessarily to have a scene for its own sake. The goal is to have a relevant scene that tells you something important. Once I'm sitting down to write—which comes after having done a lot of reporting, or a lot of thinking, depending on the kind of story—I ask myself what the point is. Why does this thing that I'm writing exist? Once I know that, then I know what I can use to say that.

We are in Madrid right now and eventually it's going to be great. But right now we're still trying to figure everything out, and it's hot and we have a seven-year-old and he's not in school and has no friends here. So, today we're having this frustrating day, where we're just running around trying to keep him occupied, and get our visas sorted out and all this stuff. It's stressful and it's not fun, and I could write an email to a friend trying to explain how I'm feeling right now. I could say, 'We're living on this beautiful plaza, and when I look out of the window, I see trees and there's a playground, and there are restaurants outdoors, and it's really lovely.' That would be the most obvious thing to say, and that would be some of the material for a scene like, 'This morning we went out and played in the playground.' But if the story I'm trying to tell is the reality of the current situation, which is, 'Oh, I'm so frustrated. Things are not going well at this moment,' that's actually not the right scene for this particular story. The more apt thing would be to tell the story of how I was trying to get a passport photo, and the first place was closed, and I couldn't communicate properly at the second place, and I don't know if I got the right size.

You can do that for any story you're telling, whether it's about yourself or somebody else. If you're writing something personal, you don't necessarily need the reader to know about everything that happened. You want it to be relevant to the point of the essay or the book. Similarly with non-fiction or something journalistic, you want to figure out what you're trying to say, and then have everything fit.

SS: When you are looking at some of these pieces and pitches with your editor's hat on, and you've edited at numerous places, including at *The New York Times Magazine*, what do you look for in a pitch? Or, the other way of asking this would be, if there are people who are just setting out in this game, what do they typically tend to do wrong in a pitch, and what could they do differently?

VV: So newer writers, in my experience, have tended to send me pitches where they're just describing the thing they want to write. They're like, 'I want to write about this. Here are the people, here's why it matters, here's who I am.' It's often written like a business email, the language is a little formal, and they're giving me some information. We, as editors, look to the pitches themselves, actually, to understand how someone writes, and that's especially true for emerging writers, where there isn't much of a body of past work. I can't necessarily Google a person and see twenty stories they've written for *The New Yorker*. If they're newer, it becomes even more important to understand something about their writing style from the pitch. I think more experienced writers are aware of this, so their pitch will be written a little like what the article would read. But, emerging writers will pitch in a way that gives me no understanding of what the piece might eventually sound like.

The way it works in publications is that a frontline editor like me, a story editor, will receive pitches, but then you have to bring that to a meeting with more senior editors. Usually, the person who runs the publication gets the final say. I like publishing emerging writers. I'll often come to the meetings with a pitch from someone who is relatively new, has maybe written one or two magazine pieces before, and say, 'Hey, I really want to take a bet on this writer in this piece', and the others will say, 'Yeah, but the writing in this pitch is not very strong and we've never heard of this person. We can't find anything else they've written other than the one link you sent us, and so we need to go off this pitch to know whether they can do it. This is not telling us that they can do it.'

Secondly, to make the case about why you're the right person to write a particular piece is I think especially important when you're an emerging writer. The first magazine piece I ever wrote was for this magazine that doesn't exist anymore called *California Sunday*, and it was a profile of the first lady of California, the wife of Jerry Brown, who was the governor of California at the time. I had not written for a magazine before, but I had plenty of other experience, and so what my pitch said was, 'I'm the right person to write this because the last beat I had at *The Wall Street Journal* was California politics. I know this woman, I've written about her before, so you should have me write this.' That was number one, and the second or third magazine story I ever wrote was for *Harper's*. It was about Indian American kids in spelling bees, and I had been one of those—when I was in middle school I was in spelling bees—so when I pitched that story, I was like, 'As you can see, I've only written two stories for magazines, but I was a spelling bee kid, and I want to write about Indian American spelling bee kids.' You have to position yourself. I know there are twenty million more experienced writers out there than me, but here's why I'm the person you should have write this one.

SS: So how do you convince an editor saying, 'Look I just got this to you first, but I should still be a good bet for this.'

VV: I have a very practical answer to that question. Unfortunately, an editor at *The New York Times Magazine*, or *The New Yorker*, or *The Atlantic*—there are a number of other publications—is very unlikely to accept your pitch, to be honest, if you've never published anything before. The most prestigious places are unlikely to do that unless you have something very special about your connection to the story that makes you the right person. I don't say this to be discouraging because there are a number of publications that do really look for emerging writers.

There's a bit of a ladder in the publishing business, where if you've published something at *Catapult* [a now-defunct online magazine], then *The Believer* will say, 'Oh, they published in *Catapult*. That's good. That gives them some credibility.' Then *The Believer* will publish it, and then the website of *The Atlantic* will say, 'Oh, they published in *Catapult* and *The Believer*, we'll publish something online.' Then you publish with the website of *The Atlantic*. Then *The Atlantic* print magazine might be interested in looking at a pitch. So, as you collect those by-lines, you can climb up that ladder and gain credibility. It's not necessarily because editors are trying to be elitist. I think it's because they have limited time, and they want to know that they're going to be working with someone who knows what they're doing, and seeing some past publications gives them evidence of that.

SS: I have a non-fiction question about form. I think more than almost any other non-fiction writer I've read in magazines, you are somebody who really plays with the form of a piece. You published an oral history of workers and labourers around the world in *Bloomberg Businessweek*, a piece in collaboration with AI and another piece that was composed of your Google search history. Obviously, you don't come to a piece thinking about form first because content dictates form, but how do you think about form? And how do you find ways to take liberties with it that aren't always taken otherwise?

VV: If I think about the three pieces you named, it was absolutely that content dictates form, but in some ways it was also that my own constraints dictated form. You mentioned the *Businessweek* piece where it was oral histories of workers all over the world, which is one of my favourite things I've ever worked on.

The way that piece came about is that my husband had this teaching job on a programme called Semester at Sea. It's a study abroad programme that takes college kids from all over the world on a ship around the world. They're studying on this ship, but they also stop in places. So, he was teaching and I was going to go along and teach one class but it wasn't a heavy lift. And as a journalist I was like, 'What opportunity is there for me on this crazy trip around the world?' It was three or four months long and we were going to stop in Germany, Spain, Ghana, South Africa, Mauritius, India, China, Japan, Myanmar. I thought, 'Gosh, this is such a cool opportunity but there's a big constraint.'

When you're a journalist, especially someone writing magazine stories, you need to be pretty in-depth in your research. You can't really go to one place and get everything you need in three days, especially if you're in a new culture and dealing with a new language. You don't know the political context and the historical context, like the journalistic history in that place. I didn't want to just pop in somewhere and try to write some big story set in Mauritius, for example. That's when I thought to myself, 'Well, what if I do something that doesn't require that kind of reporting? Could I do something using oral history where I'm really only talking to one person and getting one person's story in each place? Because I'm using the oral history form, I need to make sure it's accurate; I need to double check things as much as possible. But I can really be reliant on one source. That's something I can do with three days in a place. I can walk around and try to find one person in each country to talk to. So that's what I did.

Similarly, with that essay I wrote in collaboration with AI, I found this AI text-completion tool called GPT-3, a predecessor to ChatGPT, to be interesting. I thought, 'Let me play around with this and see how it works.' And as I was doing that, I thought, 'Well, what is the thing that this can do that I can't do on my own as a writer?' Then my next question was, 'Well, what is the thing that I have a really hard time writing about or communicating?' And that thing for me was the death of my sister, and my grief over her death. I actually had this constraint. I had tried to write about my sister and my grief, and it was too hard. I'd never been able to in twenty years of being a writer. This essay came out of that constraint. I feel like that's interesting to think about when you're an emerging writer, or a writer of any kind, really, because we all have constraints that feel like limitations. 'I don't know how to write about my sister and the fact that she died and my grief', or 'God, my husband's making me go on this trip and I want to get some work done as an ambitious journalist, but what am I going to do with just three days in each place?' But if you treat it as an opportunity, then interesting things can emerge.

SS: I'm going to shift to the novel now. What kind of changes did you have to make, in terms of writing style and technique and mindset?

VV: Honestly, the most practical difference for me between non-fiction and fiction is that I've always been paid for my non-fiction. It's what I do for work. I've worked at newspapers where I got a paycheque and my boss expected me to write something. Then as a freelancer, which is what I've done for the past seven years, I don't make any money unless I pitch an article and it gets accepted and I write it. I have this built-in incentive to write non-fiction, and ever since I've graduated college and had to make a living, I've regularly written non-fiction. I mean it's one of the things I love, but the paycheque is also the reason why it's the thing I've done consistently.

Fiction is something that nobody's going to pay you for while you're working on it. Even when you publish a short story, for example, you're going to get paid very little, if anything. Then, when you publish a book, you also might get paid very little for that. Even if you get paid a lot, if you worked on your book for thirteen years like I did, a good amount of money spread over that time isn't a lot. There's a funny relationship between writing and these financial incentives. I've really struggled just finding time to focus on fiction and commit to it, because there's always a bill that needs to be paid. That's one thing to note.

Then on the craft level, I think, I have experienced a similar problem with fiction and non-fiction. When you get to this point of frustration that's also an opportunity, this place where you have a problem to solve and you feel despair, you vacillate between those two emotions. With non-fiction, with journalism, the thing you need to do, to crack the nut, is to just go talk to more people or go back to somebody you've already talked to, and have a conversation with them in a different way that might unearth some new information. You're relying on other people, essentially, on the external world, for non-fiction. It's about a kind of doggedness and energy, and trying and trying and trying. Because I'm largely a business reporter, I have stories where I'm trying to get any employee of a company to talk. I go on LinkedIn and I send like hundreds of messages to strangers, and one person might write back and then they might ghost me.

With fiction, a lot of the doggedness doesn't work. That kind of energy of doggedness can be counterproductive. You'll end up writing a paragraph, then deleting it, then trying another paragraph, then deleting it. What you really need to do is go for a walk, or get a good night's sleep, or see a friend or talk to your mom, or whatever it is. Then, something just clicks and you can go and write.

SS: There's a kind of tech futuristic world building you do in *The Immortal King Rao*, where you are just describing things that are systemically plausible, that seem to almost be informed by a lot of your own kind of reporting research. How did you do that? And when do you stop?

VV: That's a good question. That was so hard for me with this novel. I do bring a decent amount of reporting into my fiction writing, especially with a book like this. I would read white papers about how technology that would allow mind uploading might actually work; I read Elon Musk's company's white papers and watched their YouTube videos and read some research papers. And, when I was writing, I would draw directly from that, almost as if I were trying to describe the science in an article. In journalism, sometimes you get to a moment and you need to finish the paragraph, so you can move on to the next part of the article, and you're like, 'Put something in here.' When I don't know if it's quite true, I'll figure it out later, and I'll make a note to myself that I need to figure it out later. Sometimes what happens, and I can say this having been an editor and a writer, is you put the thing in and you forget you were supposed to change it. Later you have to change it to something that's actually accurate.

But in fiction, you get to that point and then you can just make something up as long as it sounds credible. I found a lot of freedom in that, and the ability to be like, 'Well, so here I don't know what would happen, but I'm just gonna make it up.' There's so many drafts of my novel that came before this one that look like a six-year-old wrote them. When you're reading a lot of published work it might seem like these people are writing really polished stuff all the time. But I have written material that is clichéd, or material where it's just a data dump for three pages that's not interesting. I rely a lot on readers, on friends like the novelist Karan Mahajan to read a thing and say, 'This isn't working, this is boring', or 'This doesn't seem true, this is not credible', and then I go back and fix it. So, that's my process.

SS: Was there a change in voice as well, that you had to bring about? Voice, I feel, for a writer, is sometimes internal, in the sense that you know what you're doing with the voice, even if it comes out differently or comes out the same way.

VV: For anything non-fictional I write, there's no choice to make about what the narrator is like. The narrator has to be me, the journalist, right? Then there's a question of how present I am in the piece. Am I going to talk directly about my own experience? Or, is it just going to be known, because my by-line is at the top of the article, that I'm the one telling you what's happening?

SS: I was thinking more like, even with non-fiction there are whole articles in which you can be wry, or analytical or deeply descriptive and immersive, and so on. Maybe those are elements of voice, maybe there's a distinction.

VV: For me, I feel that with my non-fiction, it comes relatively naturally, I don't have to deliberately make a choice. I just think about it the way you think about telling a story to anyone. I'm talking to you all and you're one audience, and then if I were talking to my husband, I'd be talking differently, right? It feels like there's less of a process of decision-making about voice specifically with non-fiction, whereas with fiction it's harder. I think, with fiction, you have to figure out who is the character telling the story, how would they talk?

I was really interested in one or two reviews of my novel by Indian critics, who interestingly criticized what they saw as an Indian-American worldview, that was not an Indian worldview. When I was writing about King Rao, the character who grows up in a coconut grove in India, he would say something about how he tied his dhoti around his waist, and the critic said, 'Why would you say the way they tied it? You don't need to say that. This character would know how it would be tied.' I find this an interesting, valid criticism. It's also the case that my narrator is an

Indian-American. Anyway, there is that thinking that you have to do, about who is the person telling the story and how would they tell the story. So, there's mental gymnastics happening. It's not like what is the version of me that's telling the story. It's like, first I've got to invent a character and then I have got to figure out how that person would tell the story.

SS: Is there a window that you can open up into your time, balancing all of this stuff—and how you shuttle between these kinds of work?

VV: I graduated college and my first job was as a newspaper reporter. I was spending all my time, 9–5, writing newspaper articles, and on weekends I would try to write fiction a bit. I wasn't getting much time so what I did—I know there's a much stronger culture of this in the US than in some places—was I took a two-year leave of absence from my job and went to a graduate programme in creative writing that paid me to be there. I didn't have to spend my own money. I was able to spend two years just working on my fiction without having to worry about anything else. When I got back into journalism and was working full-time at newspapers and then at a magazine, I was able to find time for my fiction only on weekends.

Until 2015, we had been living in New York and San Francisco, which are really expensive cities. But in 2015 we moved to Colorado, to the town of Fort Collins, which is much more affordable. So, for the first time I said to myself, 'I'm going to start freelancing because we live in a place where I can lose half of my pay for a year and we'll still be okay.'

That was the first time that was possible. My husband and I thought, 'Let's see how this goes.' I started freelancing and what that meant was I could do things on my own time and that made it easier for me to balance the non-fiction and the fiction writing, practically speaking. I would spend four months working on a magazine article and then I would buy myself three weeks to just work on fiction. I'd have to go work on an article again, but then I would sneak in a week-and-a-half. The more experience I got, and the better paid I got for my non-fiction work, the more I was able to take time for fiction.

The other thing I started doing was basically diversifying the kinds of things I do. I was writing journalism which doesn't pay that well, so I also started teaching and I started editing. I now do four or five things—I teach, I edit, I do journalism, and every year I apply for a bunch of fellowships and grants. Wherever you live, there are varying levels of government funding for things—keep an eye out for all those things. If you can get a small grant, it might buy you a week or a month of writing time. I've been really deliberate in trying to figure out what I can do that pays well, or that can just pay me for my writing to subsidize the other things. Oftentimes, editing is the thing I do that pays the best. There is no moral world in which that's more valuable than my fiction, it just happens to pay more so I'll do that for six months and then use that to fund my fiction writing for some time.

SS: As somebody who has both written a novel that is rooted in South Asia (although also the US) and reads a whole bunch of writing coming out of South Asia, I wondered what kind of writing you want to see coming out of this region?

VV: I don't have a great answer to that question except to say that it must be really frustrating to be a writer in South Asia interested in writing for a global audience, say the US, because there's this very restricting idea in the US about what's interesting and what's going to sell. I'm aware from reading friends' works, published in English in South Asia but not in the US, that there's so much there that's more interesting and experimental, and personal and rich, than a lot of what gets published in the US. As a reader, I want to read more of that. I would say that you need to stay true to your own vision for what you want your work to be. Hopefully, the industry changes and you don't have to change.

SS: On to an existential question about this constant quizzing of yourself with regards to doubts and insecurities that can overwhelm the writing process itself—this is the day-to-day of every writer. How do you deal with it?

VV: I think the first thing that's helpful to me is to acknowledge it, and to understand that it's an okay, normal feeling to have. Understand that it says nothing about the quality of the project or the promise of the project you're working on, or certainly you as a writer. It's easier to deal with if your mind doesn't go to, 'I'm a terrible writer and I shouldn't be doing this in the first place', or 'Maybe this means this project is a failure for me'.

I worked on my novel for thirteen years and people asked, 'So how did you keep the faith in this project and know that it was something worthwhile to pursue?' For them it was such a simple question, but I was having a really hard time answering it, in part because in my mind I was like, 'Faith, what faith?' It's not like I taught myself some trick to power through. And then I realized,

'Well, what was it then if it wasn't faith?' What was it that kept bringing me back, and I realized that it had nothing to do with this question of 'Am I going to complete this book?' or 'Is it worthwhile or not?'

Honestly, the thing that just kept pulling me back to the book is that I was dealing with one problem after another. For example, I wanted there to be this technology in my novel that allows a character to read other people's minds. How does that technology work? It could be something as simple and mundane as a technical question. I have this scene in my novel where King Rao, the main character, gets taken on this weird rafting ride with this local man. It's just this random episode in the book, and for a long time I was like, 'I love this episode, but I don't know why it exists.' I didn't want to get rid of it, so I had to figure something out in the plot or with the characters that would make that episode necessary to the book.

All these little things are actually what drew me back to the book. It wasn't, 'Okay, now I've got the faith, I'm gonna keep working on this because I have faith.' It was more like, 'God, I never really figured out that thing with that one chapter with the guy on the raft. I don't want to cut it, so what do I do to play a trick on the reader or on myself to make it feel like it has to be in the book? Let me just go and solve that one thing, and the next thing.' It's one problem after another that you need to solve, and that means you're writing every day or every week or however often it is, it means you're continuing to work on the book and then you finish the book.

I think that mindset can work really well for any number of writing projects, to keep it not to faith, because that's really hard, but to be, 'Why do I do this in the first place?' It's not because I want to make money selling my book eventually. There's a moment of glory when your book comes out and it gets reviewed, and then a week passes, a bunch of new books are out. There's not that much money or glory or anything in it. We do it because we want to do it and so I try to stay true to that.

V.V. GANESHANANTHAN

INTERVIEWED BY

SONIA FALEIRO

∼

'I am allowed to take as much time as I want'

Sonia Faleiro (SF): Sugi, welcome. I want to start by asking when you first thought of becoming a writer.

V.V. Ganeshananthan (VVG): I chose to become a writer because I loved reading, and I didn't feel that I was particularly good at anything else, and so, by process of elimination, that left writing. I read widely, and in all genres—I still read in all genres. I'll read thrillers, fantasy, literary fiction and the classics. I love to read the newspaper, a news magazine, a celebrity or health or fashion or sports magazine. As others have said before me, we write the books that we want to read, that we feel we need to see in the world. And I was fortunate to have my parents encourage me. They said, 'Sure, you can be a writer.'

SF: Your parents emigrated from Sri Lanka, and you were born in the States. Did you ever feel the burden of having to be a 'model minority'?

VVG: It's not clear to me how unusual this is, but, no, not really. My father is a doctor and I'm sure he would have been happy if I had chosen to be a doctor, in the same way that anyone wants to pass inherited knowledge onto their children. But he never pushed me to do that, and neither did my mother. They wanted good grades, and they saw reading widely as a part of what contributed to that.

SF: Outside of your family, what kind of support system did you develop, specifically in relation to being a writer?

VVG: That's part of the reason that I pursued writing via educational institutions. By studying writing, I developed communities of friends who became my readers, a network of people who had been my teachers and were supportive of my career; and, I also met my agent. There's been a lot of discussion about the value of creative writing workshops, and in my own memory as a student in those classes, the thing that was singularly most valuable, especially at the beginning of my career, was when other people cheered for me.

When I was starting to write my first book, *Love Marriage* (Random House, 2008), I was in a creative writing class. When the others read the first ten pages of my novel they said, 'This is good, keep going.' They were not ambivalent about it. To have people who understand what you're trying to do, and who tell you to keep going, is important. Also, they are themselves trying to do that, so it doesn't need to be an individual sport; it can be a team sport, which I prefer anyway. I'm fortunate to have many people, specifically South Asians, who are delightfully, brutally blunt about what they think about my work, and are also a hundred per cent like, 'If you don't give me that next chapter tomorrow, I will be angry with you.'

To give you an example, I was rewriting the draft of my second book (*Brotherless Night*, Random House, 2023) and I would write more or less a chapter a day, and at the end of the day, I would send it to a Tamil friend who had emigrated from Sri Lanka, and who had lived through the time I was writing about. She would then call me up, not that much later, and tell me everything that she liked about the chapter and also everything that was wrong with it—both with great enthusiasm. On the rare day when I did not send her a chapter, she would say, 'What are you doing? I'm waiting.' Charles Dickens serialized his work in newspapers. I was fortunate to have this curious, Dickens-adjacent process in which I was serializing my work for one person.

SF: You have studied both journalism and creative writing. What did these two areas of study contribute to your work?

VVG: I really like journalism, and one of the reasons is that I love to be in conversation with people. I like to talk to fiction writers about craft, about books they're reading, about what they're working on, and also sometimes, the way they respond to news and deadlines—their habits and culture. For a long time, my intellectual life was in a newsroom, and that noise, bustle and sociability, and the sharing of resources, was very much a part of the way that I was raised as a writer—part of what I might call my intellectual metabolism. When I worked on my college newspaper, twenty years ago, I would write a story and my editor would sit down next to me, take the keyboard, and rewrite what I had done, but would explain every single change they were making. I found journalists merciless about the material being more important than ego, the deadline being more important than preciousness.

Later I went to journalism school, which I loved. I loved the people that I met there and, in particular, I loved the teachers. A lot of what I learned in journalism school in that year—I was on an arts journalism track—was along the lines of, 'What does it mean to write cultural criticism about violence?' For instance, if you're an American cultural critic, you have to ask what Americans have done to anaesthetize violence. We come from a culture where, from very early on, images of lynching were a common reference point. This was something we discussed in school, and it was also something that I took back into my creative work, where I often write about horrible violence, and I have to think about how to do it in a way that's not voyeuristic.

SF: How do you switch between the writing styles?

VVG: It's a little bit like trying to cook dinner with a bunch of different curries; some are on the front burner, some are on the back burner; some have to cook for a long time, others cook really fast. I could be working on a novel and at the same time something else; right now I'm thinking about an essay that I want to write. I'm also thinking about who I would like to pitch that to, and I'm having verbal conversations with interlocutors, only some of whom are other writers, about that essay, and some of those people are also talking to me about my novel—the next one. I guess it's about being willing to have multiple things going on in my brain at the same time. I also read a lot and interview other writers on a regular basis. I like being omnivorous. I don't have a period of time where I do one thing and then the other. I'm always doing both.

SF: With regard to writing about violence, what would you say to somebody who was trying to capture, say, violence against Tamils in Sri Lanka, Muslims in India, or blasphemy killings in Pakistan? What is it that we need to remember when we are trying to capture such moments in our books?

VVG: What you're asking could be understood in part as a question of writing about problems and issues within one's home or community. A lot of the time that I have spent studying and thinking about this is either from the position of an outsider, or the position of someone in the diaspora, kind of at the hinge between homeland and stranger.

From my point of view, say when I read travel writing about Sri Lanka, especially when it's by non-Sri Lankans, I often find it ridiculous because it frames the place as though it has only settings and objects. It rarely includes people in a believable way or as figures of importance. Here, I'm talking specifically about travel writing, but a lot of writing about Sri Lanka and about violence, in general, that I read when I was young—things have improved somewhat since—would be a picture of an unnamed person suffering. And I would think, 'That person has a name.' It would be one thing if you asked their name and they didn't want it in there, but I would like to know, did the journalist ask if they were okay with their picture being on the page?

In journalism school, we had a brief but significant interaction with an oral historian. We did interviews, oral history-style, which was different from the way I had learned to do them as a journalist. One of the principles is that you go to the interview with your questions, but if your interviewee is taking the conversation in a different way, you let them, because they're telling you something that's important to them. You allow your purpose to be altered by the presence of other people and by the notion of care for them.

I have also worked with a lot of anthropologists. Anthropology has a very troubled history, with Eurocentric roots. Some anthropologists I know—like journalists—don't want to pay their sources, but then, what does that mean about valuing people's labour and time? So other scholars find ways to account for that. I'm not saying that I think fiction writers should pay our sources or informants—I suspect mileage varies—but it's taken as a given that journalists don't, and that that would make a story suspicious. And I do agree with that in some contexts. But, what is it, if not transactional, to go and ask someone to tell their story?

I would also say that I'm more interested in self-critique than representation. There are a lot of people in the diaspora, and maybe globally, who are interested in seeing themselves on the page. I am interested in that but it is, at least for me, not sufficient, because I feel there are problems in my community and in the countries and places that I care about. If I were to paper them over, I would be doing that for the eyes of others, for a Western audience. I'm writing, first and foremost, for a South Asian audience, and when other people like my work, that's great. I appreciate that. But it is when someone of Sri Lankan origin engages with my work that I feel I'm doing my job.

SF: We've talked about Western publishers wanting to put all their bets on that one book: the one Sri Lankan book, the one Indian book, the one big book from Pakistan. How do you protect yourself from that?

VVG: My friend Vauhini Vara, who has a new short-story collection called *This is Salvaged,* had a great thread on X talking about how her books came to be published, and some of the responses that she got from the publishing industry when she was first sending out her work. One of the responses was, 'We already have an American short-story collection that touches on many of the same themes, so I don't think there would be room for this one, although we really like it.' I feel that all of the BIPOC—Black, Indigenous, People of Colour—writers looking at the thread were like, 'Of course, someone said that.' When things are ridiculous, my best armour is laughter, and I'm fortunate to be surrounded by people with a sense of humour. If you're only going to read one book, what are you doing in publishing?

You can control most things only to a very limited extent, but you can control your own reaction and how you prioritize your work in relation to publishing. The writer Lan Samantha Chang wrote a great essay called 'Writers, Protect Your Inner Life', which makes the distinction between the writing life and the publishing life. For me, publishing *Brotherless Night* has been really valuable and it means a lot to hear back from people who have read my work. But also, I feel satisfied that I can stand behind my work knowing, in my bones, that I did everything I could to write a good book. I didn't do it for institutional recognition.

I'm in a world of primarily white institutions—for example, with my first book, my publicist was white, my editor was white, my agent was white, and maybe the whole marketing team was white. I valued those relationships, but sometimes it meant explaining myself in ways that I hadn't anticipated or imagined.

SF: Sri Lankan Tamil writing has produced some great authors such as Appadurai Muttulingam, to name just one. Is your writing influenced in any way by Tamil writers?

VVG: One of the things that I did over the course of working on *Brotherless Night* and also *Love Marriage* was to improve my Tamil. I'm a heritage speaker of Tamil, which essentially means that my parents would tell me what to do in Tamil. I can conjugate the imperative very well, although I don't have the range of vocabulary that I would had I grown up in Sri Lanka. I don't have a lot of the political vocabulary or broader vocabulary that I would have liked to have. For many years, whenever my bandwidth and my access to good instructors has allowed, I have taken lessons. I have also been reading Tamil with my dad on FaceTime. I'm probably not going to achieve the level of fluency I would like, so I'm limited as a reader, and don't always have the ability to engage with work in the original, which is what I would prefer, but I will keep working on it.

I am fortunate also that many more books are now in translation. Appadurai Muttulingam lives in Toronto, and he and I are in touch. His most recent book is available in English. I also read Shobasakthi in English. Actually, it's a mode of language study; I can read a book in English and then I can go to the Tamil version and be like, 'Okay, what can I learn from reading both versions?' I've certainly been influenced by Shobasakthi more than Ceylon Tamil writers who, unfortunately, because of circumstance and my own limitations, I haven't accessed in the way that I would prefer. I think what I'm influenced by are traditions of oral storytelling, and I'm pleased that some Tamil reviewers have noticed that my English is influenced by Tamil. If you look at my sentences they are sometimes built the way that a sentence in Tamil would be built—some of that is intentional and some is just instinct.

SF: I want to talk about *Brotherless Night*, which I had the pleasure of reading while I was sharing a house with you during a writing residency in the summer of 2022. It took you eighteen years to write. How did you develop the resilience to keep going over this period of time?

VVG: When I started working on *Brotherless Night*, I did not know that it would take eighteen years! Maybe a skill that I have—and I'm not sure why I have it—is to not overthink things before doing them, and to trust my instincts. There were people who used to ask, 'How is your book going?' and then after a while I could see their faces alter and maybe they were thinking, 'She's not going to finish it, so I'm going to stop asking.' I could tell the difference between those people and the ones who thought I would finish, and the latter were invaluable—to have those people around me was great. I am very stubborn and the more it became clear that some people thought I shouldn't or wouldn't finish, the more I dug my heels in.

I also had to consider that maybe I would spend eighteen years on the book and no one would care, and if that happened, I would have to be okay with that. I would still have to think it was worth it. And then there's the narrative of, 'Oh, this person took such a long time and produced this work of genius', and then you think about who that story is told about, who is allowed to take that kind of time. As someone from multiple marginalized identities, a woman of colour in the United States, I don't necessarily have that kind of privilege. I wanted to tell myself that I did not have to obey other people's calendars. I shouldn't dawdle, but if I wasn't writing fast enough for someone else, that didn't matter, because I am allowed to take as much time as I want. And the justification for that is not fame. It is not publishing success. It is whether the work is good.

I was also deeply angry, which was a kind of long-burning fuel. There were people I wanted to hold to account—in a way that I had learned to do as a journalist—and I thought that in this case, fiction might help. There was a considerable spirit of vengeance I experienced at certain moments, when I felt that I had been lied to about certain aspects of history. I was determined to take as long as needed to know the history and put it in this book.

SF: I think one of the reasons that a lot of emerging writers feel like they need to write quickly is because they have full-time jobs.

VVG: I come from some economic privilege, but I was raised with notions of frugality and some members of previous generations of my family had been in economically precarious conditions. So early on, I had some worry about that, and that's probably not super uncommon. Also, I think my parents were able to support the idea of my being a writer because I sold work early on in my career.

I sold both my books in the fall of 2006 because I was running out of money for rent in New York—I had gone to a journalism school programme where they had waived the tuition but I had to cover my living costs. I was burning through my savings, so I called my agent and she said, 'Which of your novels is closer to done? Let's try to sell it.' So, on a really practical level, I sold my books because I was running out of money as a twenty-six-year-old in New York City.

Sometimes I think maybe I shouldn't have done that, maybe I should have waited to sell *Brotherless Night* until it was done. I had family members whom I could have called for help—I would have hated making that phone call but it was an option. At this point in my life, I teach. Not all writers want to do that and there are sacrifices that you make in doing it. But it confers economic stability and privilege. I have the summers off, I have health insurance, I have research resources, and I have a community with my students and colleagues.

SF: My understanding is that many people in the Sri Lankan Tamil diaspora tend to have fidelity towards the Tamil Tigers. You were mad, but I suspect you also made people mad. I'm interested in the response to your book.

VVG: There are probably people who don't like my work, but there are a lot of people who do, so I look at those emails. I'm trying to say things that are principled, and if the outcome of that is that people are upset, I hope it leads to productive conversations. And, if they say things that I should hear and take into future work, then I hope I will be open-minded enough to listen.

SF: I know it's really hard for you to write. It's an extraordinary challenge for a writer to face. Can you talk about how your disability has affected your writing life?

VVG: I have a motor disability—chronic injuries to my hands that limit my typing and other motions. I often use voice recognition software, which runs on artificial intelligence, which lately I feel a little gross about. I work on a Mac laptop with voice recognition built in. All of this only works if you're connected to the internet; Google Docs has voice recognition and I think its voice recognition is the best—I suspect it's because Google is mining our data to get the proper nouns and non-Anglo words more accurately. So, I use all sorts of different tools depending on what my body is capable of on a particular day. I have two access assistants, who are undergraduates—another example of a useful resource from my employer. Last night I got a very long email and I would have liked to write back immediately, but also yesterday, in particular, my arms were doing badly physically, so I stopped myself from replying because it would have hurt. Alternatively, I could have made a voice note on my smartphone, uploaded it to an AI transcription, and then had one of my access assistants edit it—it's a process, and sometimes I don't have the willpower to do it. I have a lot of reader correspondence that I haven't attended to because I've gotten long emails and I want to write back in a thorough way but don't have the physical ability to do it. Sometimes, I just feel a little goofy making a voice memo, so there are times when I have to overcome my own self-consciousness.

I read basically 90 per cent of *Brotherless Night* to one of my access assistants. I used Zoom's remote control function to share my screen and give access of my whole desktop to my access assistants. One of them was doing the proofs with me in this way, and I just read the whole book to them, and fortunately for me, they were willing to go above and beyond to do that, and also to help me keep track of continuity.

ANUVAB PAL

INTERVIEWED BY

DIKSHA BASU

~

'I don't want politics to taint
what I'm reading'

Diksha Basu (DB): Your career spans different fields and genres; you act, write, and host podcasts. Can you talk us through your career trajectory?

Anuvab Pal (AP): I'm just doing what it takes to survive. If it's gone around the world, it's because I write in English—it's as simple as that. I started out wanting to write theatre, because I felt there was a huge colonial hangover of plays 'in the canon'. They were not written for our audiences. Mahesh Dattani was writing, Rahul da Cunha was writing, but there wasn't anyone telling 'our' stories.

I was fundamentally interested in only one thing, which was our relationship to the world as Indians. That is where my plays *Chaos Theory* (Picador, 2012) and *The President Is Coming* (Random House, 2009), and the film *Loins of Punjab Presents* (2007), came from. There are certain worlds that I wanted to get into. English theatre was a way to start but there were only two ways to go, right? I'm sure you've seen this with fiction. Either you go inward within India or you go diasporic, outside, in terms of subject or audience. If I had the facilities and the genius of Varun Grover or the bravado of Kunal Kamra I might have gone inwards. But I didn't, so I went out.

Then, because I happened to meet certain people, I got into films. So, it's been a bit of a hotchpotch of a career. Sometimes, the stand-up takes over; then the podcast *Our Last Week* came out of a very strong friendship with the stand-up actor Kunaal Roy Kapur.

Being the shallow, nepotistic sort of person that I am, I stick to old collaborators and old stories. That's how I ended up where I am.

DB: Do you feel the way you look at things has changed a lot over the last fifteen years? Where are you looking? Who are you writing for?

AP: Okay, so I'll answer that, but I want to ask you first. There is an Indian novelist outside India and an Indian novelist in India, right? So, how do you find yourself in that landscape?

DB: I started writing to make my parents laugh, to put my grandmother's life onto the page and immortalize her. I started quite narrow, like an audience of one or two and that was it. I never thought my books would have any reach. This was when I was working on *The Windfall* (2017). I was doing it for pure pleasure. The book did really well and got a lot of attention internationally. Then I wrote *Destination Wedding* (2020) and the pressure started to ramp up. I started getting celebrity endorsements. Chrissy Teigen read my book; Mindy Kaling read my book; Priyanka Chopra Jonas read my book. And, my editors got really excited; my agent got really excited; and I got really excited. Then came the pressure to create work that would get that kind of attention, as opposed to creating work and seeing where it lands.

For the last three years, I've been working on a book, which I just made the very difficult decision to shelve, because it was the result of pressure from my agent, publishers, publicists, and from myself, from everyone to write a book that would get eyes again, and that wasn't what I wanted to do. I wrote the whole thing, I edited it. It was fine, but it didn't feel completely true to what I wanted to do. It was also during the pandemic. I have two small kids, so I wasn't at my finest anyway. I just could not make peace with what I'd written even though it was 90,000 words. It probably would have sold just fine, done just fine, but I didn't feel I was being true to myself. So, I made the hard decision with my agent to shelve it, and go back to where I began, which was to write about my grandmother whom I wanted to immortalize. She died in the years during all of this. I wanted to go back and write about her, her housing complex in East Delhi. I wanted to go back to making my parents read something and laugh.

So that's what I'm doing now. Back to you …

AP: Neither Manish Acharya nor I expected our film *Loins of Punjab Presents* to become a global phenomenon. It was written when we were living in New York City for essentially a diasporic audience. I should say that a lot of films that came out at the time were rubbish. I've always thought great art comes out of two things: petty rivalry and revenge. Nothing motivates anyone more. I'm old now, but I was younger then, and I said something like, 'I hate that movie' or 'That's terrible. Surely someone can write a better story.' That's how Manish and I met. He said, 'You want to write something? What's your name?' and I was like, 'I'm Anuvab.' I remember where it was. It was at a film screening on the Upper West Side in 2004.

You know, when there are no expectations and five viewers, you live a certain way, and then suddenly you become a thing. I really found, and continue to find, India overwhelming, with the attention that any visual work gets. It either gets a lot of love or it gets a lot of hate. It's very much in the public eye, and I am not a very public person. I'm quite scared of things like that. The good thing about stand-up is that I can lie; I can invent a character.

Unfortunately, Manish passed away, and my life went on a different trajectory. The *President Is Coming* started out very much like *Loins of Punjab Presents*, as a small play; the one I wrote after that started out small as well. English stand-up only happened because The Comedy Store in London opened The Comedy Store in Bombay. So, a lot of things happened in my career accidentally.

But if you live in Bombay, the pull is always more towards mainstream things. Because every week there is something big that comes out, usually done by a friend or a colleague, and it makes you think, 'Oh, why am I not doing a bit of that?' and then you're like, 'Because you're doing stand-up in Amsterdam.' If you do two or three things, it divides your time and focus. I am in awe of people who build on the one thing they do very well.

DB: Humour is often a response to something that you're trying to run away from. In my case, when I go through phases of anxiety and depression, I try to laugh my way out of it, along with medication, when needed. But it's often an escape response. Do you find that to be true?

AP: I am a cowardly, weak Bengali man. Therefore, art and comedy are places where I can make people have conflict, without me having to go through conflict myself. I'll give you an example. I recently did a show at Oxford University, where they had this big agenda, which I think is going on all over the world. They want to tear down statues. Now, it's very interesting because the group is run by students who are beneficiaries of the Rhodes scholarship. So, they want to take down the statue of Cecil Rhodes, but they're studying at Oxford on a Rhodes scholarship. It's these ironies that I find interesting.

DB: I saw you do stand-up last, I think, about six years ago, and I came out with a strong sense of your ideals and politics, while laughing for an hour straight. That's what makes you so good.

AP: Yes, but a lot less than say a Kunal Kamra or even a Vir Das. I think they're very clear about their politics and where they want it to be, whereas I'm fundamentally confused. For example, it's very easy for all of us who are a bit left-of-centre, to say, 'We're in the middle of a fascist situation.' I've seen a lot of intellectuals say that, but I don't know personally. I'm fascinated by things that I don't know and I want to get into them.

Recently, somebody said, 'You know, you should listen to *Mann ki Baat*.' So, I heard a whole bunch and Narendra Modi could be making it all up, right, depending on your politics, it could be all bullshit. I don't know if it's true, but whoever is writing for him, understands the structure of radio narrative. It's very similar to what a BBC Radio 4 programme would sound like. So, Modi will always have an anecdote. It will be like 'Rajiv in Lalitpur was having difficulty with his UPSC exam …' And you are like, 'Oh, I want to know more.' You're in it, and then all your politics about whatever you think about Modi, is out of the door.

What I'm getting at is that I don't want my politics to taint what I'm listening to or watching or reading. If you read a Delhi book thinking, 'Oh, everyone in Delhi is just a rich prick', there would be no book, right? The discovery is a part of it.

I'm fascinated by dramatically interesting, morally bad characters. I couldn't write good characters, I wouldn't know where to take them. I wrote a play called *1888 Dial India*, which was based on a suicide hotline that got outsourced from the United States somewhere to India, because it was cheaper. It's a really macabre, bleak thing that happened at the height of outsourcing, when a call centre handled people in really disturbed mental states. They couldn't afford to have that helpline in the US, so they shifted it to India. And the people taking the calls were not trained, they were just people who may have worked at HSBC.

We did some fifty shows in Bombay in 2013. I remember rehearsing with Kunaal Roy Kapur and Kubra Sait who were horrified by how horrible the characters were; how revolting; but those characters got the biggest laughs. It goes back to what Roald Dahl said, which is that people are interested in terrible characters. Don't you think? You've got some horrible people in your books, some proper, terrible people. And they are brilliant!

DB: I love every single one of my characters truly despite their flaws; actually, because of their flaws I love them. Do you get scolded by armchair critics after the fact? I went to a screening of *Court* with the actor Vivek Gomber, and Gomber at that point didn't look like he did on screen. At one point the man next to Gomber got up and said straight to him, 'What a shit film. All these awful people.' Vivek was standing right there and the man had no idea it was him. Vivek was delighted but ...

AP: The great irony is that in *Court*, which I absolutely love—I'm a huge fan of Chaitanya [Tamhane]—Gomber was the only decent character, the only nice guy, right?

DB: It's a great film, so filled with nuance. But do you feel that these days it's harder to write that way in fiction? Do you get scolded?

AP: Yes, I do. The thing I'm finding terrifying is that when you write terrible characters, people think those are your values. The reason they want to take out sections of old British comedies like *Fawlty Towers* is because some people think that what the characters are saying is what the show is saying, whereas the point of the show is the absolute opposite. How far do you extrapolate that? Do you go up to Amrish Puri and say, 'Don't blow up India with a bomb' because he played Mogambo?

I remember Gulshan Grover telling me that he had a difficult time getting an apartment in Bombay because people thought he was an asshole, and he was like, 'No, I'm just an actor. I say lines. I don't molest people. I'm just a guy looking for a two-bedroom flat.' And the landlords would be like, 'I don't give houses to villains.' We are getting to a point where you cannot make a horrible character say horrible things.

DB: I see it in books, in which every page is trying to be a lesson, which leads to a lot of really dull literature.

AP: There's a lot of comedy now that's like, 'I'm going to tell you what I think of trans people', 'I'm going to tell you ...' Arre, just tell me a joke.

DB: Exactly, it's all very careful. Do you have big ideas about what you hope or think your work, or the arts in general, should do?

AP: The only thing we can do, I imagine, is find something that inspires us. Sometimes I think, 'Am I sounding like some old uncle? Do we not get it? Do we just not get it?' I have a hipster cousin, she's thirty-one, and I'm always texting her: 'What's new?',

'What do I read?', 'What should I listen to?' Because if we lose our sense of curiosity, we've lost everything, right?

DB: A lot of newer Indian writers are willing to circle back and do that. Not having answers at the beginning of their book, I mean.

AP: I could be wrong, but I think post 2007 or 2008 there was a severing of the hangover in Indian writing to be recognized in the West. I think as Indian writers developed their own voice, it was almost like two separate rivers started flowing. The person who wanted the Booker, etc. went down one path, whereas there's a pool of writers who are quite happy with their audience in India. The same with TV, same with comedy. There are great Indian comics who are very happy performing in Hindi to a largely Indian audience. If they go to Melbourne, they'll get an Indian audience, if they go to Oslo, they'll get an Indian audience. Then there's the other river which wants to perform for the world.

Maybe the same is true for books? Sometimes those books that are made for the world don't do that well in India; likewise, the Indian books made for India don't travel very well outside. Whereas with the India I grew up in, Vikram Seth was everybody's writer.

DB: How do you find performing in the US versus the UK or India? Do you adapt your work when you're performing or do you have a set stand-up routine—beyond the usual adaptations?

AP: Well, I think of them as entirely different audiences. If I'm performing for an urban Indian audience, it's an English-speaking audience, which is one collective. If I'm performing for a cosmopolitan American audience, filled with mainstream Americans, that's another audience. The Indian diaspora in America is its own audience with values that are very different from both mainstream American audiences and urban Indian audiences. If I end up at the APAC Center in New Jersey playing to 600 Gujaratis, the evening will be very different from the National Centre for the Performing Arts (NCPA) in Bombay. Each is its own different world.

I've realized that the more connected the world has become, the less connected it is. People have now found their own entertainment and their own cocoons. What urban India is interested in is not what the diaspora is interested in; what the diaspora is interested in is not what mainstream Americans are watching or listening to. There are celebrities that break through, Priyanka Chopra Jonas, for example. But if you are a comedian like me, bouncing around the world, each pocket is a huge difference.

I'll give you an example. The subject matter of Empire is interesting to old English people and old Bengali people. You could give audiences in Calcutta—upper-middle-class people— the same stand-up that you perform for a radio or TV audience in Britain. But you can then end up in Birmingham, with a South Asian audience, with the great grandchildren of people whose great grandfathers migrated to the UK, but who have no notion of Empire. They'll understand the weird habits of an Indian uncle; they'll know how Indians are different from Norwegians in how we behave, how we are cheap, how we are polite and how we educate our children. Those broad Indian tent poles, they understand, but the notions of history are very different. So, if you ask me whether I have a universal set of an hour that I can do in Dubai, London and Melbourne—doesn't matter who is in the audience—the answer is, 'I have not.'

DB: I just spent two weeks at a retirement village in New Zealand with my mother-in-law, and it turns out I have a huge number of old retired Kiwi fans. That should be your next destination, a retirement village in Auckland.

AP: We don't realize just how huge the power of India and Indian stories are. I was recently flying from Oslo when the guy sitting next to me said, 'You know, I spent three and a half years in Hyderabad.' I said, 'Oh, okay. What did you do?' He said, 'I set up India's first Ikea.' He was a tall Swedish man and he said, 'I speak fluent Telugu', and he did, and he said, 'It was really hard to set up Ikea because we didn't know how to price it, and it's become a big hit, and we have one in Noida now, and I might be going back to India to live there.' Then he told me that he loves Jhumpa Lahiri. And he said, 'I'm a huge fan of the comedian Kanan Gill.' Incredible!

SUKETU MEHTA

INTERVIEWED BY

MIRA KAMDAR

❧

'We are engaged in a global
war on storytelling'

Mira Kamdar (MK): How did you come to write *Maximum City: Bombay Lost and Found* (Penguin, 2004), and how did publishing the book change your life?

Suketu Mehta (SM): I wrote an article about the Bombay riots in an issue of the literary magazine *Granta*, which came out in 1997—it was about the Shiv Sena. The article attracted the attention of a number of publishers, including David Davidar at Penguin India. He said, 'Suketu, I would like you to turn this into a book.' I said, 'I am happy to, but not for what you can pay me,' which would have been an Indian advance of, at that time, maybe twenty thousand rupees. He said, 'No, no, I know that, so I am going to speak to my buddy Sonny Mehta at Alfred A. Knopf.' And much to my surprise, I got a two-book contract from Knopf, and a number of publishers around the world, for a book on Bombay and a novel called *Alphabet* which I had been writing—it's a tale told by a foetus and it's still gestating. Then Sonny Mehta said, 'No, do the non-fiction book first; it's easier to explain.' I thought I'd go to Bombay for a year or two, and write a quick and dirty book about a quick and dirty city. Well, seven years later the book came out. So, my first lesson in writing a book is that books always take more time than you think they will.

I moved with my family to Bombay, as readers of my book know. I didn't know what kind of book I would be doing; I had no idea how to write a book having never written one before. I thought I'd start with going back to the people about whom I'd written the piece for *Granta*—the Shiv Sena cadre—and take it from there. I knew I wanted to get into the different worlds of the city, but most of all, I wanted to see what it would be like to go home after twenty-one years, when Bombay had grown up to become Mumbai. Beyond that I had no idea. So, I just wandered out into the city and listened to anyone who would tell me their stories. It was about where I found gripping yarns. The city was incredibly generous in offering up its stories to me.

For two and a half years I collected stories on my laptop, and in my notebooks. Then I went back to New York and got a small studio apartment in Brooklyn and spent the next three or four years writing and editing. The first draft of *Maximum City* was 1,667 pages long. When I sent it to Sonny Mehta, his assistant was afraid of putting the whole damn thing on his desk—she spread it out in a series of smaller stacks. He came in and looked at it with distaste—there was something Himalayan about it. He stopped speaking to me for nine months and then cut it in half. I still have half the book with fully finished chapters that have not been published.

I had no idea what was going to happen after the publication of the book, whether it would be a success or not. And I kind of doubted that it would be, because I remember the editor of the Bombay edition of *The Times of India* saying to me at a party, 'Now why would the Knopf readership be interested in a book about Bombay?' I responded, 'You're editing the Bombay edition of *The Times of India*, don't you know how fascinating this city is?'

But when the book came out, it was a finalist for the 2005 Pulitzer Prize for General Nonfiction. I think that's partly because there was a hunger to know about the lives of people in massive megacities in the developing world, whether Bombay or Karachi or Kinshasa; cities that are bigger than entire countries and have complex cultures. And what I tried to do in my book was combine really solid research—I spent lots of time in the city's dusty archives—with stories of people that I met, with my own memoir. It's a very personal book. It's a story about looking for home.

I think that caught the attention of readers, and people who won't give a shit about Bombay otherwise read it because they liked the storytelling. It was an approachable way of satiating their curiosity about global megacities. I also had the help of an international all-star team of collaborators, Sonny Mehta and David Davidar. When I was editing the book, Sonny did something very smart. He assigned the poetry editor of Knopf, Deborah Garrison, who is a fantastic poet herself, to do the line editing. Line editing, as anyone who has written a book knows, is like trench warfare. Line by line you've got to decide what lives and what dies, and that took quite some time.

MK: Such a great quote, 'Line editing is like trench warfare!' *Maximum City* came out in 2004 and, fifteen years later, in 2019, you published *This Land Is Our Land: An Immigrant's Manifesto* (Farrar, Straus and Giroux, 2019). I assume that in those years, life happened, as we say. I wonder if you could talk about how writing and life relate to each other, and what the reality of the writing life is in your experience.

SM: So, for the past eighteen years, Mira, I've been cooking a lot.

MK: You're a fantastic cook, I have to say.

SM: The book came out and my life got upended. I got divorced. I had to begin all over again. And I embarked on another really stupid and foolish project. I remember telling friends after *Maximum City*, 'There's no way I'm writing another book about a city again. Only if I get very drunk!' Well, I got very drunk, and signed a contract for a mammoth book about New York, which I have been writing since.

This Land Is Our Land is actually a busman's holiday. I took a break from writing the New York book by writing a quick, short book about immigration because I was outraged at the way migrants are depicted around the world. The other big project is life—it's raising my two children who are adults now; it's paying rent. I teach at New York University. I don't live in an ivory tower with an inheritance to support my writing. When you write books, you have no idea how much of a toll it will take on you. It takes more time than it is supposed to, and in the meantime, you can't stop living life. But the sacrifices you make enrich your writing. It might take longer to do a book but that book is better for it.

There's a great poem by Faiz Ahmad Faiz which goes, 'Loved a Little, Worked a Little.' The gist of the poem is that love kept getting in the way of work, work kept getting in the way of love. In the end, like in the poem, I gave up and left both unfinished. So, if there's a poem I want on my tombstone, it's that.

The working title of my New York book is *City of the Second Chance*, because it's what the city gave my family when we immigrated from Bombay to Queens, New York, in 1977—it gave us a second chance. And when I got divorced and had to rebuild everything, the city again gave me a second chance. And the kind of people I've been meeting for my book are of the same infrastructure as *Maximum City*. I've been meeting cops and refugees and wandering poets and politicians and hedge fund people—the thing they have in common is that the city gives them a second chance, again and again.

MK: Thank you, Suketu. Now, your latest book is really a plea to look upon migration as a process that is not new. That, in the West, at least, is often a result of a colonial movement of white people going to various parts of the world. As you say in the book, 'We're here because you were there.' And it is to help people understand how positive migration is, not only for an economy but also as a societal experience, what it brings to everyone's life to have people from different places come together. The book came out in 2018 when the United States was in the Trump era and vicious anti-immigration policies and white supremacy were in full throttle, to the point where Pen America in May 2022 convened a gathering at the United Nations to talk about what writers can do. And I wanted to share a quote from someone you know very well, Salman Rushdie, who said at this gathering, 'A poem will not stop a bullet, a novel cannot diffuse a bomb, but writers can still sing the truth and name the lies. We must work to overturn the false narratives of tyrants, populists and fools by telling better stories than they do, stories within which people might actually want to live.' And it seems to me that it's something that you really aspired to do in *This Land Is Our Land*. I want to ask you about this effort to tell a better story.

SM: What do Donald Trump, Narendra Modi, Recep Tayyip Erdoğan, Viktor Orbán, Vladimir Putin and Jair Bolsonaro have in common? They are gifted storytellers. But they lie. A populist tells a false story well. The only way he can be fought is by telling a true story better. And that's why they hate us; that's why they hate writers, journalists, storytellers and truth-tellers. Because we do what they do but we do it better; because most of us, I would like to imagine, tell true stories rather than false ones. We fact check, we go to our sources, we don't make things up, we don't peddle propaganda.

But the problem is that often progressives think that the truth alone will convince people of the rightness of our stories. But the truth is not enough. It's got to be told in a way which can compete with, for example, the Johnny Depp and Amber Heard trial that the United States was fixated with. There was a survey that showed that Americans cared more about that trial than they did about abortion laws or the war in Ukraine. That's why Volodymyr Zelenskyy—who's actually a good populist, a truth-telling populist—is so effective, because he comes from the entertainment industry.

I began as a novelist, I teach journalism, but I've never taken a journalism course in my life. I have no idea why anyone gets a journalism degree other than to keep me employed. But my degree in fiction at the Iowa Writers' Workshop taught me about the principles of narrative, how word follows word in order to make a world. And I think for a work of non-fiction, whether it's a magazine article or a book, you need three things: stories, statistics and a statement. You need the human stories that will bring readers into the narrative. I mean, nowhere in the Bible will you find a passage saying 87 per cent of the people in Palestine in a recent poll said you should be nice to your neighbour so that your neighbour will be nice to you. They spoke in poetry. But the stories can remain mere anecdotes if they're not backed up by rigorous research that shows that the stories aren't just individual things that the writer has witnessed. And the two together, the stories and statistics, have to add up to some sort of statement, some argument, that you are making. Our stories need to be as entertaining, arresting and compelling as the false stories of the populists.

I was in India recently studying the Uttar Pradesh elections and I went around and met all the top political leaders of all the parties. I went to the rallies. I spoke to people on the streets. The story of the Hindutva parties are simple, direct, compelling—and false, to my mind. They peddle this myth of India as an ethnonationalist state just like the Republicans and the Trumpists in America peddle a myth of America as a white Christian state. The rise of ethnonationalism around the world is about this kind of storytelling, which is that we define our nationhood—whether it's in Russia or Turkey or Hungary or India—by a simple, unifying identity: 'This is who we are and everyone else is not us.' And that's a dangerous fiction. But it's a simple fiction and we need to come up with an antidote that is at least as compelling.

Then, on the morning of the mass shooting in Buffalo in May 2022, I was in New Orleans. I woke up and read the shooter's manifesto. He was an eighteen-year-old kid who had spent a lot of time during Covid on the internet, on groups like 4chan, and he said he killed those ten black people because he was bored. He had read the manifesto of the New Zealand shooter, the man who had murdered more than fifty Muslims in Christchurch in 2019. There's a whole echo chamber of these manifestos and conspiracies, such as Renaud Camus's 'Great Replacement' theory. There is another poisonous book from France called *The Camp of the Saints*, a novel that was written in 1973, and which imagines a convoy of people coming from Calcutta, my birthplace, to France. And this novel is on [far right French leader] Marine Le Pen's bedside. [Trump's former White House strategist] Steve Bannon quotes it as one of his favourite books. These ideas made their way into online forums like 4chan and into the mind of that really sad, sick teenager in Buffalo. And then he went out into a supermarket and shot dead ten black people. Reading his manifesto made me profoundly depressed about the country, about the world, about humanity.

That afternoon, my son Gautama, who's also a journalist, and a reporter for the *Biloxi Sun Herald* in Biloxi, Mississippi, said, 'Let's go to a second line.' A second line is a funeral in New Orleans, and this was a second line for Ellis Marsalis Jr, the finest jazz pianist the country had ever known. He was also the father of a whole bunch of incredible jazz musicians like Wynton Marsalis, Branford Marsalis and Delfeayo Marsalis.

The second line is a tradition started by slaves. It's a parade during which they dance through the streets of New Orleans with a brass band. And as they go through the city, anyone can join. This second line must have been, you know, a few hundred people. Ellis Marsalis's sons were all there, playing the trombone and the trumpet and the saxophone, and as the second line wove through the streets of New Orleans, a few amazing things happened. One, the procession reclaimed the city. We walked into the middle of St Charles Street, which is the main artery in New Orleans, and took it over from the cars—all the cars had to stop for the procession to go through. Another is that anyone and everyone joined in, because the music was so infectious we were all dancing—tourists, passers-by, homeless people. It was the most joyous funeral I'd seen. It was a celebration of Ellis Marsalis's life, and the people who were dancing on the streets of the city were black and white and

Asian, and male and female and trans, and rich and poor. It was such a lovely sight. I'm not a great dancer but there I was doing my moves and I just felt hope again that, you know, there are still traditions like this which are so inclusive, that transcend class, race and caste, gender and orientation. We writers need to celebrate this. We need to spread this news too, not just the message of hatred. We all live in a palace, the palace is called Earth, and we all have an equal right to all the rooms of the palace.

MK: You've talked about telling compelling stories but folding in the stats in a narrative non-fiction work; how do you make a work of fiction about a city realistically grounded, yet let it remain a work of fiction? And I will put that together with a question about your experience with writing fiction with your in-progress novel *Alphabet*. What are your thoughts on the two different processes?

SM: I think every journalist should take a short-story writing course, at least one semester of it, and conversely, I think, every novelist could benefit by following a journalist around. I've seen some of my fiction writer friends like Amitav Ghosh and Gary Shteyngart at work, and they do a hell of a lot of research for their novels. I was with Gary in Bombay and he had a reporter's notebook just like I do. He was walking around the city and taking notes for his novels, which are, you know, great comic romps about hedge fund people and Russians in the city. He actually goes out and interviews a whole bunch of people and then he takes their stories and turns them into fiction. For me, I know I'm on to a really great story for my non-fiction, when someone tells me a story and I realize, 'You can't make this shit up.' This is so wonderful and strange. So why make the shit up? I'd written a love story set in Paris called 'Gare du Nord' which came out in *Harper's Magazine*. It's got no research or statistics, it's just a love story set in Paris. And people ask me, 'Is it real?', and my answer is, 'A writer is a voyeur into invented lives, frequently his own.'

When I write non-fiction and go back to my editors, often I realize that there's something missing. Let's say, I have two scenes in the life of a bar girl, Monalisa, in *Maximum City*, and there's something I have forgotten to ask her in the interview, in the conversations we had about that intervening scene. I know what she's done when she was fourteen, when she was sixteen, but there's a connecting scene that happened when she was fifteen, and I haven't asked her about that, and I can't go back to ask. What do I do? I remember one of my many editors of *Maximum City* who said, 'Oh, just make the shit up. Who's gonna know? No one knows her.' And I thought about it and it would be easy enough. I could just make a very small connecting scene. Lots of writers I really admire, like John Berendt and Joseph Mitchell, have admitted to composite characters, you know, by putting in a few connecting lines. I would never do that because I have spent so much time and effort sitting with my characters, for years on end, transcribing their notes and getting every quote right. And if now after all that work, I just made something up then why not make the whole thing up and call it a novel?

I think writing fiction helps when at another time at the same desk, you're writing non-fiction—you understand the difference between the two, and I really would love to go back to fiction. I'm also, among other things, writing screenplays. I have written the world's first and, so far, only Jain–Hasidic love story set in the wholesale diamond business, starring Natalie Portman and Irfan Khan which came out in a not-so-great movie called *New York, I*

Love You. I'm also writing a screenplay called 'Manhattan Cancer Comedy Love Story'. Actually, this last semester I taught a course at NYU along with Tisch, the screenwriting school, with Sabrina Dhawan who wrote *Monsoon Wedding*. It was called 'Screen Writing for Journalists, Journalism for Screenwriters' and the class was half screenwriters, half journalists. The screenwriters learnt about research techniques from the journalists, and the journalists learnt about narrative and dialogue from the screenwriters. And also, incidentally, how to make a living, because it's far easier to get a place in a writing room or writing screenplays than it is doing journalism!

All these different things inform each other and, for me, I wasn't supported by my parents when I started doing this thing. They wanted me to go into the family diamond business. So, I had to make a living myself and I realized I couldn't just do it by selling short stories. After I came out of the Iowa Writers' Workshop, I started writing for a computer magazine. I was the humour columnist 'Dear Aunt Lanny'. That's how I began writing, and then I kind of stumbled into journalism. I always thought I'd go back to fiction, because fiction was the pure, the good; journalism was just some sort of trade stuff. And then I realized the possibilities of non-fiction, and now I do both. I tell my students, 'When you come out of NYU, I can't guarantee that you'll have a job in journalism. But if I can teach you how to tell a story, you'll never lack for an income.'

I think writers now, particularly younger writers starting out, need to be entrepreneurial. We have no idea what kind of cultural product the world is going to be consuming in the years to come. But I do know one thing—the world will be demanding stories in some form or the other. As human beings, we need to reflect on our lived experience and to tell them in stories—our stories, other people's stories.

MK: What is the writer's responsibility when telling other people's stories? And while cities like Mumbai are generous to storytellers, how can one traverse spaces that are not as welcoming, especially to those who belong to minority groups?

SM: The problem of access, right? There is the famous Janet Malcolm quote about how a journalist is a confidence artist. And it's true in some form. When you're writing a book it's not like you're filing a wire story; you're following people for years and years, and you become their friends. Most of the people in my Bombay work are still my friends. When I go back, I hang out with them. But there are going to be a subset of people that will feel betrayed and, if you're doing your job, there will be people that you will piss off. Otherwise, you are just writing public relations. How do you get trust? In my Bombay book, I hung out with a lot of gangsters, and I hung out with a lot of movie people. I told the gangsters I was writing Bollywood movies, which was true. I told the Bollywood people I was hanging out with gangsters, which was also true. The Bollywood people were fascinated by the gangsters, the gangsters by the Bollywood people; so, I was the messenger between worlds.

For my New York book, I followed a group of thirty young women—models and actresses—who operated the city's most boutique weed-delivery ring called 'The Green Angels'. They were led by a twenty-seven-year-old former Mormon supermodel, one of the finest natural entrepreneurs I have ever met. It was a story of incredible female empowerment. These young women held their own in a male-dominated world. A friend of mine who is a movie producer had said, 'I've got a story for your book. My dealer is this woman and I'm gonna send her over to your apartment.' And she came over. She was three months pregnant and she sat on my sofa for four hours that first time just talking about her life. Then, she said she wanted a movie to be made about her life. She gave me complete access to her world. I would go to her headquarters in the East Village; I went with her to deliver weed, and she, you know, sold marijuana when it was still illegal in New York, to the good and the great of the city. It's a big chapter in my New York book but a section of it came out in *GQ* in 2017 as 'Queens of the Stoned Age'.

I said to her, 'You know, when this article comes out, they're going to shut down your operation.' She was in my apartment looking out at the skyline of Lower Manhattan, and she said, 'I know.' And I said, 'You also know that there's no guarantee that this will be turned into a movie.' She said, 'I know. I always knew that. But you're writing a book about New York. It's not for the movie that I've been talking to you. It's not for *GQ*. I've been in *GQ* lots of times as a model. It's because you are writing a book, and this book is going to be around long after all these towers,' she said, pointing to the towers of Lower Manhattan. 'Long after all of this is gone, your book is still gonna be here.' I said, 'You've got more confidence in my book than I do.' She said, 'When my daughter grows up, I'm gonna show her the book and I'm gonna say, "That's your mama in the book."'

So, you know, when you speak to people, when you say, 'Tell me your story', you have to offer them something. What you offer them isn't money. Sometimes, it's your friendship. But most of all it's just your ear. We pay people hundreds of dollars an hour to listen to us; therapists, counsellors. Here's a writer showing up willing to spend years of his life listening to you for free; it becomes addictive for them. There are still people in Bombay, who when I go back, continue their narratives because they've become used to talking to me and me listening to them.

MK: Can you go into a little more detail about something you already discussed, which is, as you've spent so much time with your subjects you don't want to do a disservice to them. What do you do if you're not going to make it up? What do you do?

SM: I remember having this conversation with Amitav Ghosh about writing fiction. He says often there will be the scenes in his novel and the editor will ask for the connective tissue. And then he says, 'You know what? The connective tissue doesn't matter.' It's what, in film, is known as the jump cut; in non-fiction, if you can't go back to your interview, the reader forgives you, as long as the other scenes are compelling. They realize this is how life is. Our own lives are incomplete. Think back to your childhood. It occurs in flashes, not as a continuous narrative. When we think back to our lives, or the lives of other people, there are always missing parts and those missing parts are where the reader can enter, where the reader can have questions. I think it's very important for writers to have humility, both in life and in the writing of it—and to admit that there are some things that we don't know and will never know. It doesn't make the book weaker, it just makes it more like life.

MK: You've written *Maximum City*, you're writing a book on New York. You were born in Calcutta. Did you ever feel like going back to Calcutta to write a book?

SM: *Maximum Calcutta*, how I wish! I would love to go back to Calcutta. It's my first love. I was there for six years and I haven't been back for a while. I grew up in old Calcutta, a street called Burtolla Street, which is a kind of Gujarati ghetto. I had lived there with my extended family; my grandparents, parents, uncle, two aunts. I was spoiled rotten. My grandfather had an office on the first floor, and we lived on the third floor of this really old haveli. After we left Calcutta, everyone splintered; we went to Bombay, we went around the world, and now, you know, there are all kinds of rifts in the family. But those first six years when we were all intact; that was my childhood.

I went back after many, many years. I took a taxi to Burtolla Street. The taxi stops and I get out, and I stand at the entrance waiting to go back to this—I knew the address—47 Burtolla Street. I even remember the phone number. I've got a very bad memory now for numbers and names, but that first phone number, 332-363, I remember even now after half a century. I took a step forward and then froze. I realized I could not go back. I could only go back if either my parents were there or my children were there because, you know, the past is a dangerous place. To turn back to look at it, and the one you loved, like the Orpheus story, you will be sent back to the underworld or be turned into a pillar of salt like Lot's wife. You cannot go back into the past without that kind of moral fortification. So, I ran after the taxi and stopped it. I got back in and went back to Park Street where I was staying. I still haven't been back to Burtolla Street. I'll go someday, but I'll go holding the hands of my parents.

MK: All right, I'm going to again combine two questions. How do you compete with false stories when the true stories, even if well told, can often make some people feel like the ground is shifting beneath their feet? And, how do you negotiate the tension of writing about politics?

SM: How do we make the truth more compelling? Well, I think most of us truth-tellers or progressives or professors, we live in these universities, right, and we speak to other people like us and often people in universities are very, very smart, and have gone to very good universities. A reader, like us, studies. And we read a lot of numbers, and are obsessed with facts and figures, and we speak to other people like us.

During the pandemic, I bought a house in rural North Carolina, and I now split my time between Greenwich Village and a town called Pittsboro, which has a population of 3,500 people. I have three-and-a-half acres at the end of a dirt road, and my neighbours are half gun nuts and half yoga teachers. I am thinking of starting a new kind of yoga, you know, gun yoga! But my gun-nut neighbours are fascinating. They tell me why they think there's a cabal of satanic paedophiles that lurk in the basements of pizza parlours in Washington. That they are led by a mysterious figure in the Trump administration who speaks in Rhûn. You can't make this shit up! And what do we have to offer in response? 'No, you know, the vast majority of people are not paedophiles. Studies show that sex offenders are often unjustly accused.' You can't fight that stuff with logic. It's got to be more compelling.

When I was a kid, I read Enid Blyton and the Mahabharata. I did not read studies from the Brookings Institution. So, we have to get back to that. We should read the studies, and I read a lot of studies for my New York book, but I also read novels and go out and listen to stories. Look at Mamata Banerjee—she's pretty economical with the truth, but she can tell a story. I think she pretended to have been assaulted during a recent election campaign and went around in a wheelchair. Then she won and she hopped out from the wheelchair and danced on stage.

For my Bombay book, I hung out with the Shiv Sena. I spoke to Bal Thackeray and the cadres; I met their families. Some activists accused me of humanizing the Shiv Sena. I say this in *Maximum City,* in order to understand a murderer, we must also understand the other aspects of his life. We must understand how a murderer can also be a good father, a patriot, lover or friend. Because when we examine only the murderer part of his life, when we only look at that, we're doing a disservice to our readers. It's all about moral complexity, right? It's about Dostoyevsky and *Crime and Punishment.* That's why reading fiction helps make you a better journalist.

Now the other question about politics. It goes back to the question of the *engagé* writer. How engaged should a writer be in the politics of their time? By making their books too political or not political enough? The great Russian poet Anna Akhmatova writes about the Stalinist purges in her greatest poem 'Requiem' which starts, 'In the terrible years of the Yezhov terror …' Akhmatova's husband and son and multiple members of her family were imprisoned, and she was one of the women who spent days on end standing outside the prison in the brutal Russian winter, waiting for it to open. In the poem she is standing outside the prison in Leningrad and someone recognizes her and calls out her name. 'An old woman, her lips blue from the cold' comes up to her. She says to Akhmatova, 'Can you describe this?' And

Akhmatova says, 'Yes, I can.' 'The shadow of a smile passed over the ghost of her face,' Akhmatova writes. That's all the woman wanted to know. That's all our audience wants us to know. Can you describe this? The times we are going through? What we're going through in India? In Pakistan? In Bangladesh? In Sri Lanka? In the US? In Ukraine? It's our job to describe this. To describe it as faithfully and truly as we can. And then the readers will decide to read us or not. But our job is to describe this.

MEENA KANDASAMY

INTERVIEWED BY

FATIMA BHUTTO

~❦~

'Criticism of your writing is not a criticism of you'

Fatima Bhutto (FB): Meena, in your late teens you were the editor of a bi-monthly called *The Dalit*, which provided a platform to record atrocities, condemn oppressive hierarchies and document forgotten heritages. I wonder if you can start by telling us how you began your life in writing. Was it with *The Dalit*, or earlier?

Meena Kandasamy (MK): I'm the daughter of two academics—my mother was a mathematics professor and my father a Tamil professor—but somehow (witnessing the struggles they underwent) I decided that I wasn't going to do the routine thing. From my teens, I was very sure that school was the last time I was going to read books and write exams. The first thing I wrote was something about V.S. Naipaul. People have very different opinions about him—I value his craft and if he were alive, I'd say that we should listen to him. But I think that craft in the service of power, is not what people need, it is not what is going to change the world. So, I wrote an essay called 'Casteist. Communalist. Racist. And now, a Nobel Laureate',[4] and sent it to a few friends who replied, 'Oh, you write really well.' That's why I started writing and that led to editing, which put me in touch with people like Anand Teltumbde, the scholar, among other writers. That's where the journey started. It's a very different journey from, I think, today, when people can easily share their writing with the world.

---

4   Meena Kandasamy, 'Casteist. Communalist. Racist. And now, a Nobel Laureate.' https://www.postcolonialweb.org/caribbean/naipaul/meena.html

FB: I want to talk about the book that I discovered you through (*When I Hit You: Or, A Portrait of the Writer as a Young Wife*, Juggernaut, 2017). In 2011, you spent several months married to a man who was violent, and about the experience you've said, 'I went to the police in India. I had this nine-page complaint, literally everything that had happened to me, and the officer said, "You've written a novel."' You called it, 'An intermingling of the political and the domestic', and that's what drove you to write a novel about a young poet who finds herself in an abusive marriage. You said, 'People are talking about cow protection, but no one is talking about protecting Indian women from violence. I thought I had a political duty to talk about this, as much as a personal one to tell the story.' I found that so powerful. I was wondering if you can speak about that duty, how it informed this book, and how it informs your writing in general.

MK: My father had many preconceived ideas of what it was to be a writer. He would say, 'If you're a writer, you're the woman who sleeps with everybody in town, you wear your hair loose, and you're going to beg for money because you cannot sustain yourself.' So, that was his preconception, and one of my preconceptions was that if I wrote my own story to start with, people would completely dismiss me. They would say, 'You're a woman, and the only thing you can write is your autobiography.' They'd say, 'There's nothing she can write that is not from her life.'

But actually, the most difficult thing to write with detachment, or with any subjectivity, is your own life. Once you are a writer you realize that, but earlier, I was like, 'I'm not going to do life writing.' That's why I wrote a lot of poetry, and then I started writing fiction. I was like, 'I'm not going to put myself in this little box that people are very happy to push me into. I'm going to write about political stuff. I'm going to write about a massacre that really meant a lot to me.' (*The Gypsy Goddess*, Atlantic, 2014).

The book took me six or seven years to write, and I got married in the middle of writing it. The marriage was very brief—four months—but I realized what violence means, and things that I never thought could happen to me, happened to me. The worst part of the harassment was not the physical aspect; what I have really not forgotten is the mental harassment. The idea is to erase you as a person, to belittle you, to say, 'Oh, you're famous as a poet but that's because you're young and people are interested in young women who portray a sexual side through their poetry.' These kinds of very crass comments take away from any of the intellectual labour that you put into your work.

So, I made a promise to myself that someday I was going to write about my marriage. Even as I tried to escape autobiography, even as I tried to escape the box into which people wanted to hold me, writing this book became very important. It became personal. I realized that one of the other triggers for me was not just about people being beaten up, but the constant devaluation of the intellectual self that happens alongside. That is not a small thing, it happens on a massive level within marriages, and a lot of women go through such situations. I thought I should explore that within the confines of fiction.

FB: This erasure, I guess, is what you speak about. You write in the book, 'I knew how much my husband controlled my clothes, something I made the mistake of reporting to my mother. "Love is in the little things," she said on the phone. "Wear what pleases him. Don't stand your ground or sweat yourself on the small stuff.

Men are insecure.'" In preparing for this conversation, I watched some of your interviews, and you get asked this question—and it's so strange—'How did this happen?' and you say, 'When you're a feminist, a man gets a much greater high from hitting you. I'm taming this feminist tiger. Silencing you makes an oppressive man feel better.' I wanted to ask you about anger in the purely positive kind of raging that's required against society for it to evolve. How does that kind of raging follow you through your work?

MK: If you appear a certain way, people will disassociate you from anything intellectual or political. And one has to reclaim that space to be both. But to go back to your question, which is about whether rage drives things ... When I started out, I was attending a lot of non-profit-led meetings and gatherings, and I felt the language was so plain that it didn't actually reflect the situation or the anger of the people. News reports don't reflect this anger either, which is why I turned to poetry, because poetry let me put my anger into a certain place and come to terms with some of what I felt. Rage is great if it pushes you, but I'm not sure how good it is in terms of developing a work. You don't write out of rage. You write what you see and to make sense of a story. Rage is good if it propels you into action, if it breaks your inertia. I think what you call rage, I would call passion. If you are really convinced about something, speak about it.

FB: Do you find one form of writing more powerful in this way?

MK: In an ideal world, I would write only fiction, because it allows me a lot of time, a lot of space, and it's very comforting. You can do so much magic when you have space—with words, images, scenes, characters, dialogues, sensations. I don't think anything comes close to it. I love fiction. But poetry captures urgency. Whether it's the 2020 gangrape in Hathras or the 2012 gangrape in the moving bus in Delhi, I revert to poetry; it's not just about myself, it's about condensing a moment into something. A friend and I are teaching a workshop on political non-fiction in Tamil, and it requires a lot of groundwork. If you have a lot of time and develop your reading, non-fiction is great. You have to read a lot to be able to speak with authority.

FB: Your books are described as auto-fiction and I have always found the term strange, because all novelists I know are really writing about themselves. What do you think about the term?

MK: I called *When I Hit You* auto-fiction because I was rejecting the idea of calling it a memoir. If I had called it a memoir what would I have done with the rest of the interesting, colourful bits of my life? Where would I have put them? As for whether all fiction is autobiographical, I think fiction is filtered through the body of experience. The term 'fiction' is something I would apply to *The Gypsy Goddess*, which is about a massacre that took place in 1968. I didn't see it, I wasn't in the picture.

I think the real difference is when it comes to a question of the public. A Polish publisher wanted to publish the novel as a memoir, and I said, 'No', because then it becomes the story of an Indian woman getting beaten up, which reinforces every single South Asian stereotype about marriage, male violence and damsels in distress. For me, that was not what the book was about. The book was a literary endeavour that happens to speak about domestic violence. I said, 'No, I am not selling the rights.' Read this as a novel, read this as something that comes from a writer, don't read this as something that comes from an abused woman. That's not too much to ask. People consume books to feel good about themselves—they feel they are empathetic and compassionate because they are reading a book about a woman who got abused. My book is not there to certify you; it's not there to make you feel better about yourself.

FB: Did the abuser threaten you in any way post publication? And, in the same vein, how do we protect ourselves and others when we borrow directly from our lives even if we are writing fiction?

MK: People can't threaten you over fiction. The other thing is, I think of abuse as a phenomenon. Anybody could be him. Any man who is obsessed, privileged and wants to belittle his wife could be that person. I've never made it about one individual in my life. Even in my head, it doesn't exist as hate but rather as something that I'm trying to understand. In fact, all of my other work is far more likely to bring threats towards me.

FB: I want to pick up on this idea. There's a kind of vulgar curiosity when your work is read outside South Asia. As you say, people want to feel good or want to feel worldly or cosmopolitan or munificent by reading certain kinds of works. Is it worse or better within India?

MK: The difference is between somebody looking into your bedroom and somebody standing next to your bed.

FB: So, it's worse. I'm very sorry. You've spoken about Varvara Rao's case quite a lot, and written, tweeted and talked about it keeping you awake at night, saying, 'This is blood that's on everyone's hands.' Maybe it's all over the world, but I think in the subcontinent, poetry is a history of revolution itself. It is a field of dissent, of fearlessness against power. Is it the poet that makes poetry so radical in our part of the world or is it the freedom the form allows?

MK: Varavara Rao has been writing since his twenties and now he is in his eighties, so you can read his poems as a history of independent India, as the history of dissent within independent India. These poems were all written in the moment. They captured the Mandal agitation, the demolition of the Babri Masjid, the police oppression of the Naxalite period. He is extraordinarily brave. He was even a mediator between the People's War Group, a Maoist insurgency outfit, and the state. It's not just him, take Kamala Das, an extremely political poet who wrote about sexuality. She lived in Colombo for a time, and wrote about what was happening to Tamil people there, bearing witness to the anti-Tamil riots in 1983. Poets have their heart in the right place. I think there's something about the form of poetry itself—it's short and compact, but also memorable. There's also, I think, a political culture of poetry that amplifies what poets do, which is both against the system and a part of the system.

A poet lives an outsider's life, not to be judged by society's standards, bearing it all in order to mock society itself. With poetry I feel like I'm transparent. Sometimes when I give a talk, somebody will say, 'Oh, we are big fans of your poetry. Why don't you read your poetry?' And I'm like, 'No.' I can't switch from the person who's making intellectual arguments to suddenly baring my heart out. I cannot make that quick transition.

FB: That's a great answer. There are a lot of good things about the glory of publishing, such as being invited to give talks, but do you have any warnings for first-time authors?

MK: The first thing that I would like to say is that criticism of your writing is not a criticism of you. Sometimes at poetry workshops I tell young people, 'This poem is perfect. Just take the last two lines out.' Or, 'Everything is good. Just move this to the beginning', and they act like their writing is precious. Your writing is not your puppy or boyfriend or married lover. The best thing about your writing, and the only thing you can control, is to change it before it goes out into the world. Be proud of it, but don't be precious.

The second thing I would say is that for everything that you publish, there will often be at least three times that amount of writing that didn't make it. It could be manuscripts that you abandoned or stories you couldn't finish. That is part of the process. Everything is not going to come to completion or have the blessings of the market, or even your own blessings. Abandoned projects are meant to exist, and you shouldn't feel bad about them.

Finally, work on your writing constantly. You can't be a writer by speaking about it, or networking, or turning up at festivals. Do the hard work, get the words out. Also, on the subject of writer's block, what I recommend is working on two or three different projects at the same time. That way, if you get bored or stuck on one project, there's always something else to do. If writers don't write, they are very miserable with everybody around them. So, to keep the social peace, occupy yourself.

FB: I'm very intrigued by your experience of documenting the work of the female combatant fighters in the Tamil Eelam. How was that experience, and can you share your thoughts on documenting women's role in war and society?

MK: I grew up in a certain milieu, you know; Tamil Nadu in the eighties and nineties supported the struggle for Tamil self-determination in Sri Lanka. A lot of radical Tamils looked up to the fighters. I went and met female Tiger combatants who had survived the genocide, but were later brutalized by rape in military camps. After the end of the war, the fighters were trying to escape to Europe, and the fact that they were once at the frontline of the war was a hindrance. What skills did they have? Now people are talking about Ukraine, and the refugees from there, but Eelam Tamil refugees are still locked up in detention centres in the UK, where they are paid £1 an hour. Their living conditions are miserable, a lot of them have ankle tags. They were something in society's eyes, and then overnight they were completely mistreated, almost criminalized. It's heart-breaking.

FB: Does the inevitable burnout from your work as an activist affect your writing?

MK: No, I don't think it happens at all. I think there's no perfect writing desk, perfect writing time, whatever. I don't think that's how writers function. One of my most powerful pieces, at least in my eyes, was an op-ed that I wrote for *The Hindu* in 2016, in response to the death by suicide of the Dalit scholar Rohith Vemula. I was taking part in a protest march and at one point I was on stage, and I started writing the op-ed on my phone. I wrote 800–900 words. I was reflecting the anger of millions of people, or at least the anger of those at the protest. I was part of a moment and my op-ed was a collective response. I remember writing to whoever had commissioned it saying, 'I'm composing this on a phone, but you will get it by tonight', and by the end of the meeting, I had finished it.

FB: How did you navigate translating the works of women who were poets but also fighters in the resistance, from the language they were writing in, i.e., Tamil, into a language such as English which carries its own legacy of violence and colonialism?

MK: I don't think of English as a colonial construct, because what does English mean to people from the margins? Well, English people can be pretentious about accents, but you can also be like, 'Oh, fuck you!' You can't do the same thing with Tamil, because you realize the enormity of the system that's weighing down on you. Also, even if English is a colonial language, we've been speaking it for 300 years. This return to indigeneity project has been appropriated by the RSS and the BJP. I think English actually connects us a lot, because the second or third generation of the diaspora of Eelam Tamils speak English, more than Tamil, and for them this is their history; it doesn't matter whether they get the history of their people in Tamil or English, they still get their history.

FB: In an interview you talked about how the avant-garde experimental form is more intuitively accessible for DBA [Dalit, Bahujan, Adivasi] writers, but that the publishing ecosystem pushes us to follow a template, far more sternly than is allowed to UC [upper caste] authors. How does one reconcile with this?

MK: With experimental work, especially with poetry, you can show that you don't want to be conventional, you don't want to be read the way some people may want to read you. You can pose a challenge to the reader, but the question is, would I recommend it? I would be such a hypocrite if I didn't tell the truth. A very close friend and editor, who has been with me for ten years now, told me, 'Meena, if we use the word experimental on the cover of your book, people will not buy it. We can say anything else, but we can't use the word experimental.' Experimental is a word that keeps away publishers. It's a fact. It's not only among Bahujan writers or oppressed writers, there's a tendency among those who write experimental literature to make it so obscure that it takes away from the content of the story, or begs the question, 'Why this experiment?' The other thing I would say is that, write what you have to write, do write the way it comes out and publication can always happen later, or in another form.

FB: Tamil is a language with a huge corpus of classical literature, and I'm curious about what it is like translating classical literature as opposed to modern? Do you think there is a political side to translating classical literature?

MK: The book that I am translating now is a 2,000-year-old text, *Thirukkural*, which is very intrinsic to Tamil life and Tamil culture; it's a secular text and, in fact, explicitly anti-caste. Is that a political thing? Well, in 2,000 years, no woman has translated the text, so that itself is a very political statement, isn't it? I am also translating the erotic or love poetry of the *Thirukkural*, because a lot of the people who translated it before were under the influence of Victorian morals, so the word used for sex was 'congress'. I read that and thought, 'No, that's not what this guy is talking about. He's talking about pleasure, longing, desire.'

TAYMOUR SOOMRO

INTERVIEWED BY

DEEPA ANAPPARA

~~

'I wanted to challenge the idea that there is a single model of queerness'

Deepa Anappara (DA): I was wondering if you could start by talking about beginnings, in particular the beginning of your journey as a writer. Did you want to write when you were a child and do you remember the first piece of fiction you wrote?

Taymour Soomro (TS): I wrote from a very young age, I read a lot from a young age, and we had a lot of very different books in our house. Predictably, my father read a lot of biographies and thrillers, and my mother read very, very widely. So, I would read anything. And being creative was really enjoyable for me. That kind of creativity included everything from making things physically to writing little plays, poems and stories. I don't remember the first thing I wrote, but it's also difficult to separate all of that from getting praised at school and getting praised for writing. Is it the case that I always wanted to write or is it the case that I got praised for it? I just wanted more praise. But I wrote a lot when I was a child.

Then I went to Cambridge to study law, and that was down to my sense of what someone who thought they were clever and wanted to be important, should do. I thought, 'Hemingway didn't go to school for an MFA.' So, either I know how to write, in which case, I should be a writer, or I don't know how to write, in which case, I shouldn't write. I did law, but I hated it. I kept writing and writing, but my writing was really concerned with stylish prose and not at all concerned with story. I would just write lines of what I considered very stylish prose. I sent some of it out to

157

The Mays Literary Anthology which publishes students from Oxford and Cambridge, and of course it was rejected.

I left law after a couple of years, and tried writing a novel and found it difficult. I didn't know what to say and how to say it, and I didn't know how to give a piece shape or momentum. But I also thought I was brilliant, so I sent my work out and got those very standard rejections, and then felt traumatized because it had not been as easy as I had expected. Then I did a million other things before finally coming back to writing. I must have been in my early thirties when I started thinking, 'Life is short. I should do the thing that matters.'

DA: Many writers have day jobs that don't involve writing or teaching writing, but that 'other' work still seems to shape their writing. I'm thinking about Vikram Chandra, who's written *Geek Sublime* and who talks about the links between writing and coding, and Catherine Menon who is a novelist and mathematician and said something like, 'Constructing a sentence is like constructing a mathematical proof.' Did your other jobs influence your storytelling?

TS: I think there was probably something in law, because I had to write very, very efficiently. There's no superfluous language, and I had to think very carefully about meaning. I think that was useful, but it was also less counterproductive in that I was taught to never include myself, that I should be absent from the text. So, when I started—or rather restarted—writing creatively again, I would get responses like, 'Oh, we don't know how anyone is feeling here', and I had to force myself to think about and to write interiority.

When I was in my twenties, I really didn't know what I thought about anything; I didn't have a perspective on my own life. I was constantly concerned with how I looked in anything I did. For instance, how did I look in something that I wrote? It's very difficult to write something effectively when what one is primarily concerned with is self-image. So actually, living a little gave me a bit of distance from myself in some ways.

My grandfather taught me farming, which was an extraordinarily difficult experience, but it gave me an insight into myself and into the way I thought about the world. That was critical for me.

DA: Returning to the subject of beginnings, could you talk about the beginning of your novel *Other Names for Love* (Farrar, Straus and Giroux, 2022)? It starts with a beautiful description of a journey, an emotional journey but also a physical journey, that points to the kind of transformation the protagonist Fahad is about to undergo. Because beginnings can be notoriously difficult, I was wondering, did it come later or was this the beginning for you while writing the novel?

TS: I wrote many beginnings for about three years. The novel begins with Fahad when he's sixteen years old, and he and his father go back to their village in Sind. In many of the earlier iterations of the novel, the novel began with Fahad as a forty-something-year-old man going from London to Karachi. I kept writing this beginning and then it wouldn't go anywhere. I think, in fact, you and I talked about how it was the stereotypical immigrant novel beginning; of the immigrant returning to their homeland. I was horrified that I had just written exactly that same beginning that I had read so many times! So, I thought, 'Okay, let me begin in the past, let me begin with the protagonist as a boy experiencing trauma, and I'll reorder the novel later', but I didn't end up changing it.

I remember taking that journey on the saloon with my grandfather when I was a child, and being told, 'Oh, you have to close the shutters because there are dacoits outside.' I love trains and it felt like a really meaningful place to start. It also felt technically useful to have father and son together in a confined space, and I think that the opening with the father calling out to his son and the son refusing to hear him, felt like it set up the novel. It made complete sense to me, because the novel concerns itself with the distance between a father and a son, one reaching out to the other at one time and the other reaching out at another, and their difficulty crossing that distance between them.

DA: Another technical aspect I thought was interesting was how you chose not to write certain events as scenes. How did you decide what to show and what to summarize?

TS: I would like to say that I just knew, but I didn't at all. It was really a matter of trial and error, because some scenes were dramatized and then cut. My approach was to write and then rewrite a number of times, and to develop momentum within the piece. I wanted the force of the narrative and plot to take the reader through each section, and that had its own logic in terms of what would fall away as extraneous and what would feel necessary. This is a very roundabout way to say that I don't know!

DA: You mentioned you wanted to carry the reader along. I feel that in your writing, there is reticence, or what we call recalcitrance, as a formal feature, in that there is quite a lot that you don't reveal. I was wondering how you developed that confidence as a writer, the confidence that the reader will stay with the story even if everything is not spelt out.

TS: I remember a mutual friend telling me, 'Put everything on the page, and then you can remove what you don't want.' I completely disregarded that advice, although it was good advice. I end up putting too little on the page and then having to add later. But, what ends up being really interesting and really truthful for me, is the extent to which we are opaque to ourselves. Like the parts of ourselves that we don't know and don't see, or that we don't acknowledge or refuse to acknowledge. What we conceal from ourselves ends up being really interesting to me.

Thinking of things like queerness and race, and the way that I have engaged with them, has meant that often through my life there were parts of myself I did not want to look at, that I refused to admit existed. That ends up being this project of learning, and of knowing oneself, when we are changing constantly. That project really fascinates me. The way that intersects with intimacy with other people, like how can we be close to other people when we refuse to know ourselves, or show ourselves, or acknowledge ourselves. In a way, that was really the project of the book.

DA: We have often talked about the burden of representation that we have as South Asian writers. There's a tendency in the Western world to say about Pakistan, 'This is a barbaric society', or to use stereotypes like, 'Men in Pakistan, or Muslim men, are savages.' I'm wondering how you approached the portrayal of violence in your novel.

TS: It was something I was really concerned about. These representations of Muslims, of brown men, as barbaric, misogynistic, violent, for me, felt problematic. This is not to say that they felt untrue, but they felt as true as a statement that could be about so many men anywhere, and unconnected to brownness, and to me, to Muslim-ness. So, it was really important that this book should not feed those stereotypes.

I suppose a way that I wanted to do that was to present this western perspective in Fahad's mind, and through Fahad. So, Fahad sees this place as barbaric, as uncivilized, and judges it. That was also the way that I felt about our farm when I went there. I thought, 'Oh my goodness, these people are so dirty and so primitive.' My experience on the farm was such a necessarily valuable, humbling experience, and showed me all of my own prejudice and hubris. That's also what I wanted for Fahad. It was important to me also that violence should not originate from a character in a way that a reader could read the book and say, 'Oh, this is speaking about a kind of endemic truth or a social truth.'

DA: Definitely, that. Maybe I am reading too much into it, but I felt that your descriptions of the landscape are so vivid and so stunning that it countered some of the brutality. Also, there are moments of tenderness between the characters as well, and for me that acted as a sort of buffer, or stopped me from making stereotypical assumptions about a community as a whole. I don't know if that was something you did deliberately?

TS: Thank you. I mean it's difficult to say, looking back at a book to examine it technically in terms of what techniques I consciously employed. I'd like to say that I did so much deliberately, but it felt that so many choices were kind of instinctive, or were through trial and error, and a feeling for what sounded right, or a feeling for a balance that worked.

DA: I do want to ask you about the portrayal of queerness in the novel. Typically, in these novels, foreign countries are always the saviours, and someone like Fahad would move to the States or Britain, and then all his problems would be solved. Without giving anything away, that is not the narrative of your novel. Could you speak about the decisions you made around writing queerness?

TS: When I went back to the farm, I remember people saying that this person has a male lover or that person has a male lover, and that was kind of fascinating to me. What it said to me was that, actually, I had this very fixed, Western idea about what queerness might be like in a space like that, and what attitudes to queerness might be. I realized that they were so basic and misinformed, and there was something much more complex going on. It was really important to me to challenge the idea that queerness was invented in the West, and that there is a single model of queerness, and that model originates from there.

I wanted to think about men who love men and what that might look like in other spaces, and what that might look like when those men construct a sense of their relationship themselves as opposed to, perhaps, drawing from a Western model. Then, it was also important because, as you said, the queer coming-of-age novels I'd read were about a queer character leaving the extremist, fundamentalist, conservative parents' homeland and going to the liberal West, where they live happily ever after, and are accepted. That felt so false and reductive, and so full of prejudice against rural spaces and brown spaces. I wanted to push back against that.

DA: You've written a beautiful essay called 'On Origin Stories' in our book *Letters to a Writer of Colour* (Vintage, 2023). It's an incredibly moving essay. The reason I thought of it was because of *The New York Times* review of your novel, which seemed to have completely misunderstood its narrative. As we discussed earlier, there are certain narrow perceptions in the West about the shape such stories should take. I was wondering if you have any advice for emerging queer writers on resisting expected narratives, and on how to deal with one's work being misread.

TS: When I was in my twenties, I tried writing, and I wasn't out, and my book was bad. Then, when I was in my early thirties, I was out, and I wrote again. Now I could be honest, and truthful, and my book was good. This coming out narrative gives a lot of satisfaction to a Western audience, but it felt very reductive and simplistic. Having said that, my relationship with my parents got a lot better when I came out, so I'm grateful that I did, but I have complicated thoughts about coming out.

Coming out exists only because queerness was criminalized, only because queerness was stigmatized, and, while the Queen was celebrated for decriminalizing homosexuality, it was the British who gave us anti-sodomy laws. It feels like coming out, in a way, also relates to a surveillance culture where our sexuality is surveilled by the state. We have to declare, 'I'm not a threat'; 'I'm telling you there's a homosexual here just so you don't have to worry.' That narrative feels problematic to me, or rather, I don't want to celebrate that.

Then, when I started thinking, 'Okay, well if my story about how I've ended up writing, sort of improving as a writer, doesn't connect to my coming out and the truth telling of coming out, what could it connect to?' I talked earlier about how I was concealing parts of myself from myself, but also concealing parts of myself from other people as well. This was a constant labour that I was engaging in, and to some extent, it felt like I needed to do it to protect myself from harm. I thought this kind of lie telling, this fictionalizing and fabricating, why can't this be my origin as a writer, as a fiction writer, all of these fictions that I engaged in when I was 8, 9, 10, 11, 12, 13, 14, 15, pretending not to be queer, or Pakistani, or acting as a woman in a play, or pretending that someone straight found me attractive, those things?

I wanted to see those as lessons in fiction; I wanted to see those as the lessons that taught me how to tell stories. And, that felt actually more truthful to me in some ways than this reductive story about my coming out, sort of welcoming me into some kind of the truthfulness that would allow me to write.

DA: In some ways, it's about engaging with those parts of our lives we may not be really proud of, and closely examining something which we might think is embarrassing?

TS: It's those feelings when things are too close, when things are embarrassing, when things are awkward, when they aren't good, those are the feelings that I have learned to lean into, as opposed to the feelings where I'm like, 'Oh, this is such a beautiful line, so people will love this.' I can't speak for others but those are not the feelings for me to lean into. And, actually, the other place is the place that is much more interesting for me to learn about myself. For me, personally, what's important is that I'm a pleaser, so it's been really important for me to examine those impulses in the story I'm telling and why I am telling it, particularly when the story is very simple and very satisfying, and, particularly when the story is a trope. I think those have been signals to me: 'Is this your story? Or is this just a story that you've chosen?'

DA: How did the novel's structure, and your understanding of the characters, change through your drafts? Did you always know where the story was going?

TS: I don't plot out in advance, and in a way my drafts end up being these outlines that I make. I write a full draft and then rewrite it each time, and then I work out how this or that happens. I knew there were some things that happened in the story; I knew it was about a father and a son; I knew that it would feature their farm; I knew that some traumatic sexual event had happened in the son's past. So, in a way, I was trying to write into or towards that, but a lot of the events of the novel emerged as I was writing them. The characters emerged from those events, how they responded to those events told me who they were, and I really couldn't have said in advance, 'Oh, this will happen, and this is what they will do', because they came into shape through the writing of the novel.

DA: So, as you wrote the novel, you were learning more about your characters, and then the story changed as well.

TS: Yes, because sometimes I would have an event, and it would just feel untrue. Then, I would think, 'Okay, well they didn't do this, and they didn't respond this way.' For me, that was part of the process, taking the wrong turn and then retracing my steps. I wouldn't know, often, that it was the wrong turn until I'd taken it.

DA: What advice would you give someone trying to finish the first draft of their novel? What elements are important to get right in the first draft knowing you'll be revising it?

TS: It felt really important to give myself permission to write badly, and not to worry about prose, and not to worry about pretty sentences, and to power forward. Until I had the complete draft, I wouldn't really be able to make sense of the shape or the structure of the piece. And then I would go and write it again from scratch, from a blank page. I would say give yourself permission to write badly and just finish it. Don't worry about any of the questions, about getting the shape right, because I do think we have instincts for storytelling, and we lose sight of those instincts with the editor-in-our-voice telling us, 'Is this character right? Is that sentence right? Does it look like this? Have I got that historical detail right?'

I think what ends up being important for me, and again I can only really say this for myself, is the shape of a piece and the shape of the story that holds everything together. I would only get that when I would power through it and then start again, and power through it again, and do it again, and each time that shape would become refined. Also, what was so important was to tell myself, 'Write badly, there will be another draft. Just write anything here. It doesn't matter how the dialogue sounds, just write it. It doesn't matter, just go forward.'

DA: Can you speak about creating distinct voices for each of the characters? Do you have any advice on how to set multiple characters apart, say, through dialogue?

TS: What I end up thinking about a lot is, 'What does a character want?', and that their wants will drive their actions and their dialogue too, because their mind will be focused towards some very specific things. In our stories, we imagine their minds to be neatly joined together in the furtherance of our plot and our story, but that's not how minds are, or how people are. People are thinking about their own problems, even when they are in dialogue with someone else. They might not even be listening.

I have, perhaps, on occasion not listened to what you've said, Deepa, and answered the wrong question, or answered whatever question I wanted. That ends up being quite important to me when I'm writing dialogue, to think, 'What is this person concerned about? What are they bothered about? Are they really listening? Are they paying attention to the person that they are with?'

DA: Do you have any advice for emerging writers about what they should do once they have completed a novel, and about the publication process?

TS: It is challenging. I'm perhaps answering the wrong questions again, but there are two questions here. One has to do with revision, 'Is a manuscript ready, and is it working? And, how do we know?' As far as that is concerned, I really just got to a point with my own manuscript where I was kind of exhausted, and I had rewritten it a number of times.

I thought, 'This doesn't work but I'm done.' That was how I knew that the process was over for me. In terms of getting to publication, it is really random and difficult. In some ways, that's the wrong thing to say, but I feel there's one way of looking at all of this, which is that, 'This writer was brilliant and that's why they succeeded.' That feels very untruthful to me, because so much comes down to privilege and chance and a moment. What becomes important then, is to hold on to the value for you in the creative process. It applies even after publication, because publication can be a very brutal process. When I reflect on writing before being published, there was this joy in it because I was writing without all of these other voices in my head, with only my own voice in my head, and not the voice of my editor or agent, or the Goodreads reviewer who didn't like the book, or the *NYT* reviewer.

I wouldn't have believed it had a future-self told me this but, that private space to write is a really valuable, beautiful space. It's a space in which we can be full of insecurity and doubt—Why am I doing this? What's the point of this?—but it is also full of a kind of joy of creativity. That, in the end, is a reason we do this, and what a gift it is to be able to do this, this joy of being able to make things—which is also a huge privilege. We see our peers with corporate jobs, having their own home and all of those things, and as someone making art you have to hustle.

In terms of getting published, it's really difficult to say with any meaningfulness what it takes to get published. What can I say? Persevere and send your work out, have a group of readers that you can share your work with, and just keep doing it and keep doing it, because it is important to you, and you value it, and you love it. Before being published, I thought to myself, 'My god! I will weep tears of joy when I get my book deal and when I'm published.' Of course, I'm so happy and I'm so grateful that I was published, but it is not that you pass through this golden gateway into this beautiful, perfect space where you have no doubt about yourself and your writing, and no fears and no insecurities. It is not as difficult afterwards as it was before, but in a different way it is. I would say, keep writing, and keep making work remembering what's important to you, and sharing your work with friends, or with readers whose views are important to you, and sending it out to journals that you love, and being prepared to be rejected from everywhere, because some people don't know how to read, and some people won't like your work. It will happen.

DA: Do you have tips on how to be kinder and patient with your own work?

TS: Oh, gosh, this is so difficult! I often wonder why I am so different giving feedback to others than when I am critiquing my own work. Why am I so different when someone else tells me, 'I don't think this is good', or 'I'm struggling', or whatever? Why do I try to be so gentle, supportive and encouraging? And, yet, with myself, I am like, 'How lazy you are that you didn't get that writing done?', 'How stupid you are that you haven't written that piece?', and those kinds of things. I think that writing, art making, is difficult, and I feel embarrassed saying it because it sounds like a really privileged thing to say, but I find it really difficult. The other thing I would say is the 'not writing time' is important, and for me, a lot happens in the time when I'm not writing, but actually feeding my creative spirit just by doing whatever feels important.

Also, there's the thing that I don't do enough myself but would like to do, which is to think, 'Wait, how would I treat myself if I were a child? How would I treat myself here?' Would I say, 'How stupid you are. You're not going to achieve anything like this. This book is going to be the last book you will write.' Would I say that, or would I say, 'Come on, you did this before. If you need a break, take a break. If you can do a little, do a little. If you can do fifty words, do fifty words.' This is advice more to me than it is to anyone else, but that's the advice.

DA: I also think it's helpful to have that distance from your work before you go back and start polishing it. Then the problems become much clearer. Whereas, if you're constantly looking at it, then it's all a bit of a blur. Having that distance, sometimes even physically, just going somewhere else, helps.

TS: Yes, and having you has been so monumentally useful for me. Having you, for example, having a brilliant reader who knows me, knows my writing, knows what I'm trying to do, who can also give me some insight when I don't have any perspective on myself. I think you're absolutely right, sometimes distance really helps. I think, also, we kind of know the problem. We may not know how to resolve it, so often for me the solutions have come in those moments before falling asleep. I'm lying down and … 'Oh, that's what happens!' This tells me that sitting in front of the text is sometimes not the solution, and often for me reading and rereading is not the solution; the solution for me usually is time away, or is writing, more writing or reading someone else, but rarely is it fretfully rereading my own work.

MIRA NAIR

INTERVIEWED BY

SONIA FALEIRO

~

'Keep your eye on the prize'

Sonia Faleiro (SF): Mira, you recently celebrated the twentieth and thirtieth anniversaries of *Monsoon Wedding* (2001) and *Mississippi Masala* (1991) respectively. The longevity and excellence of your career immediately brings to mind the question of resilience. How did you develop resilience?

Mira Nair (MN): It's a question I ask myself these days, because I'm at a different stage of life and yet feeling incredibly, deeply creative. I learned about resilience at an early age without realizing I was learning it. I am the youngest child of three, the only daughter with two older brothers. My father was an IAS man in Bhubaneswar, Orissa, and my mother was a social worker. I learned many things from them, but one thing was their emphasis, very sweetly and without any big deal, on the boys. I was just the faltu at the end. I used to joke with my family that no one really knew what I was doing. The best thing about that is that I found my own way without being prescribed to.

Oral history was a big part of my inspiration. In Orissa, jatra, the folk theatre that travels through towns, was a formative inspiration. Later, I discovered that Peter Brook and the other theatre people I used to admire—because I was once an actor—had also learned from jatra. We had a cultured home. We didn't have many books, but music was important, ghazals especially. Begum Akhtar visited our house in Orissa and gave an amazing concert. These were powerful images for me growing up. Also, my father only spoke Urdu—he was a Persian scholar. In the pre-

Partition days, the men were trained in Urdu, and the women learned Devanagari and Hindi. My father was from Lahore before Partition, and my mother was from Amritsar, so we had an interesting and musical home. I studied the sitar for two years when I was eleven, and learned from my teacher that to excel one could not have many pursuits. That piece of advice was a major moment of understanding. That I could not do 100 things with excellence, I had to focus. I also study yoga, and for forty years I've been practising Iyengar yoga. I have absorbed that humility of surrendering to not knowing, to never thinking I know fully, because even in the simplest position, thought, or raga, there are volumes to know and to discover.

My focus in my teen years was political theatre. I studied with Badal Sircar who lived in Calcutta, and we made plays that were about themes important to us, and took them out on the streets. When I was eighteen or nineteen years old, I wanted to be challenged academically. Although I had a scholarship to Cambridge, I had an attitude about the British; I could not go to 'the Raj' to study. I could not go to a culture that had so fully oppressed us. I used to tell my family that if I had grown up when they did, I would have been an anarchist. I would have killed someone. A large part of making *A Suitable Boy* (2020) was wanting to live in the fifties when India was being made.

It was this pursuit of not wanting to go to England that led me to apply to American colleges. I sent off applications and six months later the postman came to Bhubaneswar with a very large envelope from Harvard, of all places. I don't know how I had the brazenness, but mostly it was to do with finding my own way. I always say that one must cultivate stamina and one must keep practising the craft. The craft is not just, as in my case, film-making, but it's arming yourself with knowledge and community. We don't realize how important a creative community is. I am grateful to have always cherished my community, so that even thirty or forty years later, I can rely on some people to speak the truth. I don't ask too much too often, but it's important to know that I'm not alone.

I wanted, right in the beginning, to bring the unseen to my story. I never saw people on screen who looked like us, who did what Ashima Ganguly did in *The Namesake* (2006). She had no idea how to dress in the snow and wore her husband's overcoat over her muslin sarees. I wanted to make my distinctiveness my calling card, and never let them forget it. This is why I never let them mispronounce my name. I say 'Nair' is like 'fire'. 'Near' is not my name. Now the world has woken up a bit to needing to learn; now they're ashamed about how they said our names, but I don't let them forget. I tell television anchors before we start, 'This is how to say it.' So, a long-winded answer, but I hope you get a sense of how it is.

SF: What I found most fascinating about that answer—not at all long-winded and full of all the right amount of details—is how you spoke of a career being made by challenging oneself, refuelling and learning. There is however the question of rejection, which is also a part of the creative life. Has that affected you?

MN: I never used to feel that I didn't get what I deserved, because I have a sense of pride. *Mississippi Masala* was a really radical film with a big movie star (Denzel Washington) but it was turned down by Cannes. Cannes is one of the pinnacles, one of the temples of our industry, and I had been a big hit at Cannes with *Salaam*

Bombay! (1998). So, it came as a shock when *Mississippi Masala* was not accepted.

I didn't want to admit it to myself but today I do admit that the treatment of people like me by the temples of cinema was not commensurate with many of my male colleagues. The path to recognition, and even reward, was not equal. Now everyone is on the back foot trying to make amends—it's a mandate now in our industry to hire women, to hire people of colour. I don't buy it. One of the phrases I use is, 'Don't drink the Kool-Aid', which means don't buy it because we are the flavour of the moment. Continue to believe in what you do and how you do it. Continue to raise your own standard among your own community of people. Never feel complacent—complacency is death. That's why I talk about stamina, craft and rigour, these are the pillars that must not change. They are difficult to sustain, at my age, which is sixty-four, but I'm full of energy and vibrancy.

SF: It sounds as though it may have been lonely at times. Were you afraid?

MN: I did not fear. Fear is paralysing; I would not recommend fear, it will not help you in terms of the creative act. The loneliness, for sure, but one thing, Sonia, that I really recommend, is to never lose your sense of humour. Humour is important to confront the backlash you will get from a hundred people. I also had what I call 'the foolish confidence of the Ivy League'. When you've gone to places like Harvard—I only have a bachelor's degree—you develop foolish confidence. It was my foolish confidence that led me to Denzel Washington to whom I said, 'Hey listen, I have an Asian interracial love story that no one else is going to offer you. Sit with me?' And he did, but only because he loved *Salaam Bombay!*.

And that's the other thing I want to say, which is that the quality of your work will open doors for you forever. Keep working until you know it's as you want it to be; not to please others, but to have it as you want it to be. This is one of my pet peeves about friends in Bombay. Great film-makers would ask me, 'How did you make *Salaam Bombay!*?' It was such an internationally distributed film at that time, in 1988, when Indian films, even Satyajit Ray's films, were never seen in the world. They would come up to me with stories of what they thought were international but were really just imitative. What is sometimes missing from us is rigour. The first draft should not be fucking published. It's about pushing yourself and sharpening your skills, we call it 'spitting and shining'. You have to keep doing that and subject yourself to opinions. Be receptive, don't be high-handed.

Many times, Sonia, in our movies, the bigger the budget, the larger the committee that you have to listen to. It's a team sport. That's the other issue, how do you navigate the whole world's opinions, and then your own? I am here to tell you that sometimes it's not possible. Sometimes you can't preserve your own ideas, and you learn from what others tell you.

SF: India is undergoing a political and social transition that is crippling creative people. What do we do when we are faced with such a challenge? And how do we find joy when the world seems bleak?

MN: Your first question is the question of our times. At one level, it can appear like it's all right but lurking underneath—I am thinking of the scorpion—is the forever possibility of several bites to come, either at once or staggered. Many writers are at the frontline in terms of dealing with it and I would have loved to ask you that question, because I am sometimes protected by my comings and goings between India, Kampala, and where I move. I don't run away from things but it can get heated up. Like two years ago, when we went back to India, my husband Mahmood [Mamdani] and I were concerned that we would not be allowed in. I remember joking when I got the Padma Bhushan—I was making *The Reluctant Fundamentalist* (2012) at the time—and someone from the Home Ministry called. I thought it was a prank. I said jokingly, '*Haan, haan, haan*. Am I getting a shawl, a piece of land and the promise of no arrest?' He said, 'Madam, it's the Home Minister calling.'

The daggers of our struggle now are constant. It's not just Hindu–Muslim, it's so much more. The only thing I can say for myself is that it furthers my grit. Just last week I was speaking to the great Iranian director, Asghar Farhadi, who made *A Separation* (2011) and I was saying to him that we admire the Iranians, how they deal with censorship in cinema, and how they find interesting ways to do it. He said, 'I hate that I have to obfuscate, that I have to find another way. I do not believe in it and I cannot do that.' But what he does is very interesting. On the surface, *A Separation* is about two people negotiating a divorce, but in the revealing of it, the film reveals everything about Iranian society.

It's similar to writing about Amrita (Sher-Gil), in trying to bring her to the screen, which is the project I'm working on. She challenged all norms with a strong moral compass. Her artistry came first, but she navigated what it was to love men, to love women, to understand her own Eastern heritage with her flamboyant Western cultural teaching. How did she navigate all these threads into making not just her life but her art? The art that

lives on so extraordinarily and represents—the term is overused—
'us all'? She brought colour to the canvas in a way that had never
been seen. For me, it's still about working in a way which, without
being preachy, holds the mirror to the world. Young women and
men are still confronting challenges in terms of who to love and
how to love. The challenge is how do you keep your eye on the
prize, the prize that helps you, which, in her case, is painting, and
in my case, film.

As for the second part, about what brings me joy. When I
started on this path, I used to love reading biographies. I still
do, of people I loved, like Billie Holiday and various artists who
had given me succour and refuge. So many of them had ended
their lives in madness like Van Gogh. I thought, '*Mera kya hoga,
yaar*?' Will I go insane? Long story short, early on I decided
that my family, my relationships, my loves, would always be
the most important to me. They were not always familial—they
were creative collaborations, friendships. I made that decision to
honour, cherish and love, and, as the struggles of life happened,
that family became my buffer; so I am devoted.

I have a family of two boys, my husband and my thirty-year-old
son, and it's not touchy-feely like, 'Hi mama, what will you have?'
but it's a beautiful compass. I take it seriously. For instance, what
gives me joy is Thanksgiving, because it's about cooking and not
commerce. It's about gathering. We just celebrated it last week
and my joy was two or three days of cooking with my family and
a close friend—just that one constant of having food and a door
wide open. We feasted, we danced, it was bindaas.

I also nourish myself with art. In America, it's artists, and in
India, it's Humayun's Tomb, Khan-i- Khanan, Hazrat Nizamuddin,
where I live. In Kampala, I am a gardener. I have built a garden,

partly with my film school, Maisha, which has a mentorship programme, and every student and every teacher plants a tree in my design. Now it's a forest of thirty-five-year-old trees. Everything grows there. The Line of the Equator runs through my garden, so it's very fertile. Then there's Iyengar yoga. B.K.S. [Iyengar] used to say that 'yoga is the stilling of the fluctuations of the mind', and I long for the fluctuations of my mind to be managed somehow so that I can work.

SF: That was gorgeous, thank you so much. Let's now talk about stories, and how you choose which to work on.

MN: When you're looking at your work, it's important to not think of a notion of success, or what some other person has. A small case is when I was making *Indian Cabaret* (1985). I was sharing an editing room with Spike Lee because neither of us had money. He worked for twelve hours and then I worked for twelve. He was making *She's Gotta Have It*, and it became a big hit. I told myself, 'Spike can have it because he's a black kid in America, and has a community. I will never have that community, and I won't have that community even in India. So, I shouldn't mess my head up with "that success" becoming my success.' These days we're flooded with yardsticks of success—this prize, that prize—but it's important to sift away the fruits of one's action. As the Bhagavad Gita says, beware the fruits of action, because it's confusing to think about the fruits when you're doing the action.

As for choosing stories, it's sometimes a matter of intuition, and sometimes serendipity. *The Reluctant Fundamentalist* came from being invited to visit Pakistan. We went there, Mahmoud and I, and were embraced by the culture. I was inspired, in terms of the love, the largesse, the music, the refinement, the depravity—it was everything. When the book came along, which I was given about six months after my trip, I thought, 'Here it is!' It's about this guy who loves America, and who makes this journey, and asks, 'Why this love?' For me that was an instant fit. I knew it would be tough but I just had to tell it. So, different films come out of different states of inspiration.

SF: One of the noticeable characteristics of your films is how even minor roles are treated with great care. Like that of Alice, the maid, in *Monsoon Wedding*.

MN: Alice was actually the Adivasi maid in my brother and sister-in-law's home. The remarkable thing about the real Alice was that one day she complained of a stomach ailment, and when my sister-in-law took her to the hospital, a baby was born! Alice did not have any idea, she was sixteen. In *Monsoon Wedding*, I wanted to make an upstairs-downstairs tale, because we live upstairs-downstairs in our part of the world, and often don't know anything about Alice's world. That was how Alice was born.

At first the attention was more on P.K. Dubey (Vijay Raaz) who was going to be a gadget freak. He was the new India—we shot the film in 2000 when beepers were getting popular. In the casting of Tillotama [Shome], who was a young kid in Lady Shri Ram College, things changed. Vijay and her had a chemistry that was very powerful, especially visually. Alice had extraordinary dignity, however little she earned, her dignity was foremost, which was beautiful. Alice and Dubey represented non-material love, what in our old texts used to be called 'gandharva vivah', the marriage of the flying spirit.

SF: Music plays an important role in your films. Can you talk about the process by which you choose your soundtrack?

MN: If I love someone's music, I'll go to them. I loved Vilayat Khan saab, so I found Vilayat Khan saab. He turned out to be in New Jersey and I became his friend. He did the music for *Kamasutra*. It was the old days where you bring the guy to the screening room and show him the film. I remember dying of nerves. It was a pretty erotic film, it had nudity, but he saw it and said, '*Aapne to hamare desh ki haar banai hai*. (You have created a jewel for our nation.)' I was like, 'Wow!' Then he took out his sitar and performed 'Jaijaiwanti' till 5 a.m. in the studio. The lesson of that was, 'Ask people you'd love to work with', because the worst they can say is, 'No.' But if you don't ask, it's already a no.

When we were working on the story of *Salaam Bombay!*, Sooni [Taraporevala] and I used to hear L. Subramaniam's 'Raag Kirwani' not even knowing I would later use it. I had never made a feature film at the time, I had never worked with a musician, but we were listening to this very haunting raag. I listen to music very carefully and never as background. I listen to a lot of Indian classical music. So, 'Raag Kirwani' was the haunting melody I listened to while the story was being written. Long story short, I went to L. Subramaniam, who had never done a film before. He was quite dazzled by the fact that he was asked to do music for a movie. I sat with him for six weeks, and we extrapolated things he had already recorded to things he was going to record for me, to hit the frame in a certain way. Same thing with *The Namesake*. There was a great boatman song, 'Bhatiali', that Nitin Sawhney made, which became the foundation for *The Namesake* soundtrack.

Again, Nitin had not done narrative music; he had done his own records which I loved, but we made a beautiful track.

Now I'm more assured with music, and it's a very close and, sometimes, very delicate collaboration with the musician at hand. But I really enjoy it and I think it's a great part of film-making. It's a real privilege to use music in this way. It's important to get the rigour. One thing I can't bear about our current South Asian cinema is the emphasis on what they call 'background score' but which I will always spell as b-e-g-g-ground because it's a manipulative thing that tells you how to feel. There's no silence in any of it. A large part of using music is using silence to hear the music or to listen to what the music can do.

I make my own tapestry of sound for a project and it keeps me going. When life is tough with the project, I listen to the music. The same with *Reluctant*. 'Mori Araj Suno' was originally sung by the great Tina Sani, but I made a new version with Atif Aslam, and that song kept me going for five years while I was raising money for the film. I am basically a student of ecstasy, I love to be ecstatic! I like to go into that, and music is the way for me. Find the music that keeps you burning and surrender to that.

ALICE ALBINIA

INTERVIEWED BY

TARAN KHAN

❧

'The madness of the effort
is an important part of the
process'

Taran Khan (TK): I thought you could start by talking about the idea of travel. Did you think you were writing a travel book when you started researching *Empires of the Indus* (John Murray, 2008)?

Alice Albinia (AA): I thought I was writing a history book! I did a whole master's degree at School of Oriental and African Studies (SOAS), which I tailored to be about the Indus, because I knew I wanted to write about the river. I'd been living in Delhi when I got the idea to write the book. But I also knew that I needed to do a lot of research. I wanted to touch the river. So I flew to Karachi and went and looked for it. Everybody was so surprised. They said, 'Where is the Indus around here? There's no Indus left.' Suddenly, this book that I thought was one thing became something different.

I found myself writing a book that involved a lot of journeys. I resisted the idea of a travel book for a long, long time because they seemed a bit rubbishy to me. But, to be honest, I just love going on journeys. I love going on historical journeys in my head and in libraries, but I really, really love being a voyager.

TK: Which brings me to my next question. Travel writing is a magical literary space, where one can insert oneself in a way that is trickier than with non-fiction. How do you decide how much of you goes on the page?

AA: The Indus is a really long river, and therefore, each chapter required a different approach. I put myself in to describe a journey that I took or an encounter I experienced. Mostly, I felt like I was writing other people's stories, and I put myself in only as a vehicle for their stories. But it's true that since I was writing the book, my encounters were important. At the moment, I'm finishing a book about Britain (*The Britannias: An Island Quest*, Allen Lane, 2023) that's similar to *Empires of the Indus* but it's written through islands, which is a different geographical conceit. Again, there are chapters with a lot of storytelling, but I also found it useful to tell the story through how I encountered that material, those places and people. My next book of non-fiction is set in the nineteenth century, so I can't be there, which is great.

TK: Let's talk a bit about how *Empires* took shape. I remember you talking about how thoroughly you worked on your proposal. How did you handle the tension between research and being out in the field, where nothing goes according to plan?

AA: I found writing non-fiction book proposals before beginning to travel very helpful. In both cases, travelling along the Indus and around the British islands, my proposal has been a real anchor for me. Sometimes I can turn up in a place, and feel, 'What am I doing here? I can't remember why I'm here.' That's happened to me in remote islands and on remote bits of the river bank. That's when I can say, 'Well, I'm here for Chapter 12.'

In my case, I did all this research beforehand, and then went to the river, and it became a different book; much more ecological and a story of modern-day people. But, I was always balancing. I would try and fill my mind before I went, be it around Britain or through the Indus Valley. Before each journey, I would fill my mind with historical data, and the books that I was carrying with me, and poems. But there's a limit to what you can keep in your head, obviously, just like there's a limit to how fast you can write in a notebook.

With the kind of books that I write, the proposal is really useful because it reminds me that I can't put everything in. Obviously, a book is going to be richer for the more information that goes in. In this way a book is like a river. There may be lots of sources and tributaries but there is one river, and you have to find your way through it, narratively. The proposal is really helpful in that sense, because it's the narrative thread, the river. You don't want to get lost for too long with the tributaries. You've got to get to the sea!

TK: That's a great metaphor. Once you've done the research, what tools do you use in the field?

AA: I record a lot. I like recording people talking, obviously, but also noises and songs. I think that first journey is always so useful, for showing me what I may not have seen. There's always something one hasn't seen, or quite understood. Therefore, being in a state of openness to what is going to be shown, is really helpful.

I loved buying notebooks all the way through Pakistan, and I remember that when I was back in Britain writing up the book, I would have the notebook that I bought in Hyderabad, and the one that I got from Chitral ... They were a memory palace.

TK: When you're recording things, are you doing it with a sense of how it will work for the book or are you trying to figure out how it will fit?

AA: It's a bit of both, because it's always exciting to find something that you haven't thought of, and you know is going to be the thing that you've been looking for, and is going to take you through a chapter. But, there's also a lot of searching and not really knowing, in my case, anyway. I think it would be really great to come up with a streamlined process. That's kind of what the proposal is doing. But also for me, there's a lot of looking around and listening. I don't know what the percentage is, what goes into the book to what the research is, but there's probably a massive disparity. I'm sure it's true for you, too, isn't it?

TK: I found what you just said, which is that you cannot know things, really liberating. It's not something I heard a lot when I was writing my book (*Shadow City: A Woman Walks Kabul*, Vintage, 2019). It's fine to not know what you're listening to, or even why you're listening to it. It may or may not fall into place later, but spend the time, waste the time, maybe run out of questions to ask. Spend the extra day in the place, be a little bit bored, let people get bored with you. And, how do you balance the importance of getting everything right while listening to people tell their stories? There is an innate tension.

AA: When I was finishing *Empires*, I began to doubt everything I had written. I wrote a piece for *National Geographic*, which was a nightmare to fact-check, because there was a village I had been to, in Sindh, Pakistan, which I was told was called Rahim Khan. The fact-checker at *National Geographic* said to me, 'There isn't a village called Rahim Khan. Did you mean this other village?' And he gave me a slightly similar but different name for a village that was about

200 kilometres away from where I'd been. And I got the map, and worked out, 'We'd gone along this road, and stopped here', and eventually, thank God, I rang up a friend who lives in the Thar desert and is a Sindhi speaker, and he rang up someone else and then he rang back and said, 'Alice, it's Muhammad Rahim Khan.'

Take as many notes as possible, and just assume that your mind is going to play tricks sometimes. Check all the sources you quote from. It's really wonderful how people speak; they speak so poetically, and recordings are so useful, not just for fact-checking but also for the poetry of everyday language.

TK: I think footnotes are really useful to accommodate some of the contestations you get over things when you're in the field, because there will be different stories. But the recognition that there are many stories is key to the process of writing about different places. Once you've finished travelling and you're back, how do you actually write?

AA: The thing I find most helpful is writing with a pen or pencil first. It's something alchemical about the brain. Putting words down in a way that you can play with them on the page—I always try and do that, before I take it to the laptop. Then I take printouts. I do a lot of editing and I love cutting words. I get such joy from slashing paragraphs. For me, the first draft is really important to record on paper. I don't often look back at it, but the process is a fruitful one.

TK: You have a job, you have young children, you have other writing commitments. What is your secret to getting the words on the page?

AA: It's so different with fiction and non-fiction. I found with fiction, I could just write anywhere, I could be in a cafe, I could be talking to someone. I don't know why and I wish somebody could tell me. Whereas my process with non-fiction is different. *Empires*, which was my first book, came out of me with some ease, maybe because I had recently graduated from university, and I'd been writing essays and working as a journalist in Delhi. Whereas this new book about Britain has been written after I became a mother and with a lot of different things going on in my life. Finding the time to sit and write was often painful, in terms of clearing mental space. It took a lot of effort to step away from my home and family, and find somewhere within myself.

It is an effort you have to make. I always write so much better when my phone is physically distanced from me. I don't know whether you have any insight into the kind of mantra you need to say before you begin writing non-fiction. I think it depends on what else is going on in your life—a lot of it is mental. It's about finding the tranquility you need; to go back to that river metaphor, to float down that river while ignoring the different people calling to you from the banks. You have to find some inner peace sometimes; and that's really hard. Also this book has been so slow, the one I'm just finishing.

TK: *Empires* was a lot quicker?

AA: Well, actually, no. I'm hoping one day to write a book that's really quick!

TK: There is something to be said for the mechanical process of just turning up every day, switching on your computer, or opening your notebook and writing. What I found was that writing residencies really helped, because then I was completely away from my own environment, and was only expected to work. Talking to other people can sometimes also open doors. I remember listening to a visual artist describe how he had created a series of works, and that led to an 'aha' moment for me at a time when I was blocked. It can also be helpful to step away from the text. There is a benefit to doing other things as long as you are able to tap into them for your writing. I also took a long time to finish my book, and I'm glad. It would have been a different book if I had written it quickly, which was also an option. Once you're returning to it and rethinking it, and looking at the connections, it takes shape quite differently. Do you agree?

AA: I think I probably work better out of my home, and after having a bit of exercise. I cycle into Central London, disgusting and polluted though it is, and just that bit of exercise helps. Finding your place to write, which is somewhere that isn't familiar, helps, because it's easy to get distracted in familiar places.

TK: Let's talk about editors and readers. How do you find a good editor, and who reads your work first?

AA: I love being edited. I think partly because during the long process of researching and writing the book, it's always just me on my own. But it's contradictory. Getting lots of people to read your book is obviously good. But you've got to hold on to your sense that this is your book and it's your mind that has created this work. But there's also a point at which you have to let go, and a book becomes a communal process.

TK: I agree that you do have to hold on quite firmly to your concept of the book. Especially in the initial stages, it can get very confusing if you share it widely. But I've also found it enriching to have other authors read my book. It's been really helpful to have close friends who are also writers, or good readers, send back their thoughts.

Let's now talk a little bit about passport privilege. In *Empires*, you were able to travel to places that people with South Asian passports cannot. How is it to write against that absence, to be able to do things or not be able to do things, depending on where you are from in the world?

AA: I had massive passport privilege while writing my book on the Indus, because until I went to Pakistan, I didn't realize that, for example, Indian journalists came over on a 'city visa'. I had never heard of a 'city visa' until I met an Indian journalist living in Pakistan—it's such a crazy idea. I was lucky I had a tourist visa, and I wandered around even more than maybe journalists were able to. I also found it helpful being a woman. I wasn't expecting that when I went there, but there was a privilege of gender also. I could talk to men, and then I could go and talk to women who wouldn't have been able to talk to me had I been a man. Search for the privilege you have. There's also language privilege, depending on what part of South Asia you're from.

I see all the places I can't go to, all the conversations, religions or cultural nuances that I don't understand. What I would say is, 'What is it that you can use about yourself and your situation?' Because if you go deep enough to that aspect of yourself, you can bring to a book something that's going to reveal wonders. It's going to be wonderful, the bits of writing that come out of that particular aspect that's unique to you. How did you find it in Kabul?

TK: Yeah, it was also a privilege, but it took a while to recognize that. I felt extremely welcome, which I had anticipated but not to the extent that it happened. I would agree with you that you have to search for your own perspective and recognize it as being worth investigating. Write against the absence, which means that you write what you see and recognize that your story has power. Also, how does one know which ideas are worth pursuing, from a commercial standpoint—because a non-fiction book requires some time before an editor can be approached.

AA: Well, I also write fiction which takes absolutely ages before one can approach an editor. So, to me, non-fiction is much quicker, in that you write a proposal. My first proposal was 10,000 words; my second proposal was 30,000 words, which is almost a quarter of a book—that's pretty long. With *Empires*, I went a bit crazy. There were journeys I went on that I didn't tell anybody else about and places I took some risks to visit. It's good to enter a state of slight madness when writing, you have to do that. The process of writing this book about Britain has been very different because I've travelled with my two small children and I couldn't do anything I wanted—I was responsible for other people. But it's also good to push yourself to the end of what you think are the limits. The madness of the effort is, for me, an important part of the mystery of the process. I think finding your vein of madness is probably good, but recognizing that maybe you shouldn't really have done it, or just saying to yourself, 'Okay, that's enough now', is also important. 'This book has got what it needs, and it's time to stop.' It's good to know when the end has come, isn't it?

My next book is going to be short and quick, because I'm going to be really, really organized about my field notes. I'm going to have a completely anthropological approach, and everything is going to be coded; there's going to be a red section, a yellow section, a green section. (*Laughs*). I am determined to have at least examined this approach before deciding it's not for me. What did you do? Any really good organizational tips?

TK: I wish that I had known before I wrote the book to annotate as I went along, rather than leave it to the end. Put your references in when you're doing the work, because doing that at the end is not fun at all. That's the most bitter learning experience I had from my first book. Recently, I have come to embrace taking photographs and recording audio. This wasn't really possible in 2011 in Kabul, but it's a lot easier now. I prefer to move around without technology getting in between, because I find it easier to take handwritten notes, rather than have a Dictaphone or telephone between me and the person talking. I learned to report at a time when you only had a notebook, so I am quite good at keeping eye contact and taking notes. But that means I do have to go back and organize them later. So, I like the analogue way of doing things because there is a tactile sensation to it, which helps me remember the moment. I'm not sure I can make the transition to anthropology, but I do feel that when I'm researching, it definitely saves me from burning up a lot of my blood and sweat later, to be more organized at that point.

NILANJANA S. ROY

INTERVIEWED BY

MARIAM TAREEN

~

'It might be beautiful, yes, but
is it true?'

Mariam Tareen (MT): I'll start by asking about your first novel, *The Wildings* (Aleph, 2012). Could you take me through the process of writing it?

Nilanjana Roy (NR): Through my twenties, there was no question of finding the time to write a novel, even though I had multiple ideas floating around in my head, simply because just earning a living took up so much time. But in my thirties—I finished *The Wildings* when I was thirty-seven years old—I quit publishing because I realized I was meant to be a writer more than a publisher. Most of what had held me back, and I want to be honest about this, was simply the fear of being seen, of being out there as a writer, and not as a journalist or reader. I really had to work to get over that.

The Wildings made it easy. I had been writing short stories of all kinds and some of them were stories about the cats in my neighbourhood. Most of my writing happens with my feet; I take a walk and the stories start to flow on their own. *The Wildings* came from making friends with cats, then discovering, as I followed them around, that their lives were teeming with action, adventures and unlikely friendships. There was a fair amount of research, because I had to make that leap out of the human universe into a city that was fascinating but distinct from the city I knew so well—an undercity, almost, in Delhi's Nizamuddin. But I didn't think it would be fair to have cats walking around as semi-human characters, even if I'd translated their unspoken feline communications into human dialogue for the purposes of the book. I felt it was only fair to create a universe that worked for cats; we are seeing the world from their perspective, three feet off the ground, not from a human height. It's a chiefly nocturnal world, so my entry point into it was through the main character, Mara, who is both curious and fearful about the outside cats.

I did relatively little outlining for *The Wildings*; at that time, I believed that the best way to write a book was to let it come to you. I did do a lot of character sketches—there are scores of cats and cheels (brown kites) and mice in the book—but I did detailed character sketches for the five or six main cats, and the rest of it, I thought, I'd let it come to me. Big mistake. Some writers like Arundhati Roy can write a novel sentence-by-sentence, letting that strand take them through. But I realized—belatedly!—that I am an outliner. I do better with a plot and structure laid out, and once I do that, the imagination can float around wherever it wants to. I feared an outline was going to be a cage, but it turned out to be much more freeing once I had the timescale and plot down. After that, I just had a lot of fun.

MT: How much did the characters change from outlining to when you started developing the story?

NR: I took a lot of time to build a world to begin with, and my first draft of *The Wildings* was about 800-pages long, and had to be broken into two different novels. A lot of hectic side-plots vanished, mercifully, but the characters evolved. Mara, who is the lead character, is scared of the outside world because of a tragedy that she witnessed right after she was born, and she spends a lot of the novel battling her fears. Most of our neighbourhood cats communicated through their whiskers. They sit there and quiver at each other in a benign or sometimes mildly aggressive way, or sometimes when they are more agitated, their whiskers vibrate like guitar strings—you get a big show. But because I know cats pretty well—I know a lot of the neighbourhood cats in Nizamuddin personally—I tune into whatever world it is I am building, whether it's human or animal. Once you learn to let go of human preconceptions, and you let yourself observe without judgement, then the cats unfold this complicated world of alliances and threats, of species that live side by side, and of the constant need to fit oneself into a world built by and for humans.

I remain fond of many of the characters in *The Wildings*. Katar, for example, who is one of the clan heroes, was based on a very serious cat I knew well. That gentleman made it his business to take care of the cats of Nizamuddin; he had a permanently harried expression on his face because none of the queens and toms would listen to him—they were busy doing their own thing. Miao was based on a real and beloved cat who became a good friend; and Mara was strongly based on the first kitten who adopted us. But as happens with reality and fiction—and this is true of fantasy as much as it is of fiction—once you get it on the page, things change.

Their voices developed in a way that will be familiar to anyone who works with realist literary fiction. You have to quieten down, and you have to get your preconceived ideas of what a character should be and do out of the way. There's a lot of listening involved.

All of us have pretty chaotic lives; and we have families, jobs and friends, and the rest of the whirl of life. But for me, most of the writing happens when I can quieten all the way down. In that still space, once you hear the voice of a character, it's unmistakable.

And then there's just the question, 'Is that it, exactly?' It's a bit like with friends; it takes a while to figure out who your friend really is. You may think you know a person well, but it's only when you listen, pay attention, that you can anticipate every shade of how she's going to react. It's the same with fiction. If you give them time and space, your characters will come to you.

MT: I've heard many writers talk about writer's block. Would you have any advice on how to get unstuck?

NR: I don't want to sound mystical, but almost always, when you get stuck, it's because the spirit of the story has faltered. By the spirit I don't mean anything esoteric. As readers, when you love a book, you're tuning in to the life in it, and as writers, when your writing becomes forced, or mechanical, or the fictional world is unclear to you, you've lost your connection with the spirit of the story itself.

A block often happens when you try to do too much too fast, and you just need to take a break—don't be scared of that. Artists and architects, other creative people, do that all the time; they see it as part of the process. Don't make that break too long, but during that break don't force yourself to write. Go off and do something completely different. A lot of writers work with their hands in some way or the other. Anuradha Roy is a potter, Jeet Thayil draws, Shehan [Karunatilake] and Jeet are musicians, Kiran Desai and Siddhartha Mukherjee like to cook, and some of my friends like gardening. Doing something with your hands seems to help clear a block.

I cook, or walk, or paint furniture. It's soothing, that whole process of sanding down a trunk and then applying layer after layer of paint and varnish on it. Somewhere in the middle of that work, you understand that what you're trying to do with the writing is similar. Maybe one layer is wrong and needs to be stripped off. Or you have to let go of the desire to hold onto something that you've created when you know it isn't working. With my novel *Black River* (Context, 2022), I cut about 180 pages—when you discard, learn to let go with as little regret as possible.

MT: What comes naturally to you as a writer? And what's your least favourite thing about writing novels?

NR: I was the kind of kid who either had my nose buried in a book or I was wandering off exploring neighbourhoods, climbing trees, crossing Palam airport, trying to track down random jackals whose calls I'd heard from the fields. Delhi was a small place in the 1970s. It's not surprising that the muscles that I developed were the muscles of the imagination. This has come maybe too easily to me—I really did not get it when people asked the classic, 'Where do you get your ideas from?' question. I couldn't compute, because all through my life, like a lot of writers, my mind generates an idea a minute when I'm not actually working on a column or story. The imagination is not a problem for me—but corralling that, by which I mean, bringing some order to that chaos, and choosing and settling down with that choice, is difficult.

The biggest question for me as a writer has often been, 'What kind of a writer am I?' I struggled with that a lot because I didn't have a voice, really. I was a glib, good journalist; I was great at getting people to open up, not so good at investigative and hardcore, factual stories—I was never much of a news journalist. But I was fine so long as I was following the rules, writing in someone else's voice. And voice is so much connected to character, personality, to being willing to show up as who you are. The struggle was to stop people-pleasing, to write the book that I wanted to write, in my own voice. I really had a lot of work to do, where that was concerned.

Over time, in my case, I have had to learn to be dexterous. I had a fixed idea, drawn from many interviews with writers, from reading *The Paris Review* interviews, or talking to Indian writers, of how one should go about the writing day. And this day would start in sanctity. You would light an agarbatti or lamp or something suitably luminous, have mellow respectable music—writerly music—in the background, and fresh from yoga, sit down with ink and paper, and go about your work. That's not the way it happens.

Okay, the agarbatti part often happens because I like setting an intention for my day's writing. But the rest of it, usually, you're writing around corners; you're writing in the middle of juggling fifty other things. And even when you have that gift of a block of time in which to work, often you spend hours staring off into space, because something is coming to you, and you're not yet ready to write it down. And even when you're ready to write it down, that first draft will need work, and so will the second, and you have to find the patience, beyond the skill and the pleasures of the imagination.

We are always looking for the shortcuts, the magic, the secret sauce that will somehow get your book written. And the fact is, the moment that you shift perspective to, 'I want to finish the work', 'I want it out there in the world', whatever it is that your goals are, you start to put everything that you know and everything that you're learning into the service of that particular book.

MT: That's lovely. I was reading a review of *Black River*, and the reviewer wrote, 'Roy's success lies in the fact that it is actually comforting to read her work, not just for the clarity, but also the beauty it generates.' I found that to be so true. How do you find that balance between writing sentences that are beautiful and getting on with the story, and getting all the technical aspects right as well?

NR: That's so generous, both of you and the reviewer. The beauty: I can't take credit for that, it comes from the world of *Black River*. It's not a classic murder mystery—I have a feeling most people will figure out who the murderer is because the choice is limited. But it is about the aftermath of a murder, about a certain kind of careless power and about painful absences. It's about piercing grief, but at the core of *Black River* is the unlikely friendship between three strangers to the big city, Chand, Rabia and Khalid, who find a kind of freedom on the banks of the Yamuna. It's a record of a time when those friendships were possible, as we're moving towards an age when those border-crossing friendships seem more and more rare, almost forbidden, along with many other things. Perhaps what happened was I allowed myself to be vulnerable on behalf of the characters, but also for my own sake. So, maybe the beauty that people perceive in the book came from that source.

Black River was written over a five- or six-year period; most of the time was not spent writing. Some of it was spent on research, and some with my father, who passed away in 2021. He was intermittently ill, so I took long, long breaks from the book, as one does. I think I spent about three-and-a-half years actually writing the book. To break it down—about six to eight months was spent on research, much of it walking along and learning the life of the

Yamuna, the Aravallis, the outskirts of the city and Delhi's slums near the giant landfills. And a full year was spent on learning technique, even though I didn't understand that was what I was doing at the time. I kept trying to write scenes that I didn't have the skill to pull off. One thing I wanted was for people to be able to read it really fast, to finish it in a day if they liked, but also to be able to come back, and read it slowly and find greater depth in it. You don't choose a title like *Black River*, if you're not going to follow through.

Books have their own life once you're done with them, but I'm happy that I did justice to everything that I saw so vividly in my imagination. And, I think, I did justice to what the characters wanted, in a strange way. While they were fictional, they placed a lot of trust in me. We don't have a background in common, and that was a concern. Then, as I grew to know their world better, I grew convinced that I could write about their lives with respect, and I could honour those lives. That part I'm comfortable about. I see things now that could have been done better, a sentence turned a certain way that could have been turned in another way. What I'm trying to teach myself is to be a little bit more honest with every book that I write, and to let the book convey that honesty.

Sometimes the work was agonizing, or emotionally demanding. It seemed impossibly hard, in the same paragraph or same chapter, to write in such a way that the reader could speed through it in 30 minutes, but also to write so that if a reader wanted to slow down, go back, reread, there's something more. I felt an urgent need to try to capture some of the changes I saw in the bloodstream of Delhi and of India: a hardening of attitudes, a widening crack in the city's long history of assimilation, but also the persistence of caring in a time of deepening heartlessness. This is a clamorous time, and in an age where everything seems to happen so swiftly, fiction becomes a kind of memory keeper.

I think there's a reason for every book that you write, and that reason goes beyond merely wanting to be an author. There's a reason why the book you're writing came to you. Many cultures believe that tales find their tellers. Girish Karnad, the late playwright and novelist, one of India's greatest writers, and the American novelist Elizabeth Gilbert both believe that something mysterious happens, that a story chooses you. Don't be afraid if a piece of writing, even one to which you've given much time and attention and care, dies midway. Maybe you can revive it, but if you can't, it's okay. Perhaps it taught you a few things about writing, but it wasn't your story. But it is a milestone when you find your story, whether your book is serious or light-hearted, when it's truly yours.

You need perspective on your work. A hack that I often use: I'll print out my writing in a different font, and go large on the font size, say 13–14 points. It works. But never read your writing with tired eyes. When you finish writing something, step out, walk, talk to friends, whatever. Refresh your mind and ideally give your writing a gap of a few days before you read it. My amazing agent, David Godwin, has read every first draft that I finished, and he handles my impatience superbly. You're always unwisely in love with your own work and five minutes after I've hit Send, I'll be all, 'David, this is ready to go out and meet the world.' David is very gentle about it, 'Of course, I'll get back to you in a few days.' And what he's actually doing is giving me time to call him back four days later to say, 'David, please don't send that to anybody right now. It's terrible, it's atrocious, it's a horrible piece of writing, and I need to work on it.' We need perspective on our work, and perspective takes time—it can't be rushed.

MT: How do you know when you've reached the right point at which to end?

NR: I didn't have a problem where *Black River* was concerned. The ending was visual, and it was so strongly felt; it came to me and I held on to it. I resisted the temptation to go beyond that point of stillness and solitude. But this is a delicate thing and depends very much on the kind of book that you're writing. If I have a choice between one of two endings, I like to break it down into scenes. Take two sheets of paper, no more than that, and write down each ending in some detail, two sentences, three sentences at a time. When you've entered the world of your novel successfully, you will typically want to overwrite. And be careful about too much neatness. There is a natural, instinctive ending to a good book; it's felt deep in the bone. If you're confused about how to close, go right back to the start of the novel. Take a couple of days off, and read your entire book out loud to a good friend. Not quietly to yourself; read it out loud, every sentence, every chapter. At the end of that you will be exhausted, and your friend will be at the end of their patience, but you will also have reconnected with the beating heart of your story.

Be wary of the epiphany ending, whether it's a short story or whether it's a novel. It's a shimmering place to land on, and often we are very much in love with a beautiful line of dialogue, a transcendent image. But what you have to ask yourself concerns that eternal balance between truth and beauty in the novel. In this case, it's not, 'Is it beautiful? Is the orchestra swelling in the background? Is every violin and every sitar strain heard?' It might be beautiful, yes, but is it true? And that applies to every genre—you could be writing romance, you could be writing comedy, it doesn't matter. When it's true, you know for sure. Sometimes, you're ducking it because the truer ending is actually the harder one to write.

While writing the closing chapter of *Black River*, I wasn't ready to let go of that world. It was sad in a way I can't fully explain. It's like watching people you care about move to another country, promising, 'We'll be right back.' And you know that you won't meet them again for decades.

VINOD JOSE

INTERVIEWED BY

MIRA KAMDAR

'We are not in a newsroom,
we are in a war room'

Mira Kamdar (MK): Vinod, I have a memory of being on the roof of the Delhi Press building in 2010. I'd come in from New York, and I'm there, you're there. And, it was very rudimentary, physically, with plastic chairs and all, but the atmosphere was electrically charged. It felt like something important was happening. I wondered if we could start off by having you talk about this founding moment of *The Caravan* in 2010. You'd just joined the year before, I think.

Vinod Jose (VJ): It was the end of 2008, when I was in New York, that Anant Nath—the grandson of Vishwa Nath, who founded Delhi Press in the 1930s—reached out and asked if I would return to India and help launch his grandfather's magazine, which had gone off the shelf sometime in the 1980s. On the one hand, I was very excited about the offer. At the time, for a journalist in New York, the feeling was akin to standing in the middle of a cemetery of dying newsrooms. The financial crisis, the loss of credibility of the legacy media after lying about the Iraq war, and the rise of the digital media, had contributed to print institutions folding up, or scaling back. People passionate about print journalism didn't know where to go. In that sense, it was a great opportunity, but I was on a different journalistic path.

In the summer of 2008, after graduating with a master's in political journalism from Columbia Journalism School, I had started working as a radio producer in New York. Radio was my passion. But if you moved between the homes of the many writers and budding writers living in New York City, there was little chance of escaping the long-form narrative journalism bug. An American publisher was happy to give me a decent advance to develop one of my long-form pieces on Burma into a book. I was already drawing up reporting plans.

The job I was offered was to launch India's first long-form narrative journalism newsroom. Building the team, fine-tuning its vision, and leading the editorial development of the magazine would mean giving the magazine a certain kind of personality in craft and content. My journalist friends in New York joked that I would be one of the last editors in history to get an opportunity to shape a print publication in the twenty-first century. Finally, I came to the conclusion that I would launch the magazine, run it for a couple of years, and then say goodbye to write books. It was in these initial months of taking up the job at *The Caravan* that I met you on the roof of the Delhi Press building. I was already neck-deep with the task of putting the building blocks together. We had set the deadline of January 2010, to hit the stands with a new look, and deep and exciting narrative pieces.

There was also a reason why I would get in touch with journalists like you. Initially, I was under the illusion that I could get all the editors and long-form writers from the Indian English journalism ecosystem. But long-form editing and reporting were not valued in Indian newsrooms. Editing, as Indian print newsrooms understood it, meant fixing the language—editors looked at grammar, changed the text to a certain house style, etc. They did not edit for content or structure. And reporting came out of a very short intellectual engagement with a story. The reporting language was in the cryptic, 5W1H format, of arranging information to the questions of what, who, when, where, why and how in the inverted pyramid format, the typical formula set by the newspapers and news magazines. Often, these reports were written in the announcer's tone, the typical tone of the newspaper language. There were not many reporters who stayed with a story for long. Either their editors pushed them to the next story, or the reporters did not want to get stuck to a story, and moved to the next even if they knew there were holes in the reporting.

Moreover, on the craft of reporting, the rigid rules of newspaper journalism made sure there was very little room to experiment. From the number of sources to the elements of reporting, reporting for scenes and hints of characters were almost impossible. The closest place to experiment with form was the feature desk, but not with hardcore political, business or social stories. Even in *Outlook*, regarded in those days as the leading Indian magazine, reporters would work on a story for maybe three days, or a week. To talk to forty-fifty sources and if need be, go to 15,000 words, was absent in the making of a newsroom's conversation in India, until *The Caravan* came about.

Most journalists in those days were talking about *Open* magazine, launched a few months before us. One of India's richest industrialists, the owner of power companies and tea and rubber plantations, had invested a few hundred crore rupees to lure a large number of journalists to work for him. *Open* purchased billboards across India, and hired the best designers and support team. The mismatch of resources was massive. I felt like the gang leader of an impoverished band of street urchins. But our stories, especially the cover stories, were big, ambitious, well-rounded and well-written.

By 2011, on a cover-story-to-cover-story comparison, we had beaten the top two magazines, *India Today* and *Outlook*, in reach and in conversations generated. During my fourteen years working in *The Caravan* from 2009 to 2023, there were over one hundred journalists I got to work with full time. Creatively, it was an exciting period.

MK: The idea of *The Caravan* as an Indian *The New Yorker* is one that I remember being a way to help people understand what it was you wanted to do with the magazine. I mean you guys came out swinging. Could you talk about some of the stories you think of as the most important that *The Caravan* has broken?

VJ: We started at the end of Manmohan Singh's first term, which was a period of high political excitement for the Indian establishment. There was the nuclear deal, which announced India's arrival on the world stage, forcing the United States to change its strict nuclear laws to accommodate India's growth appetite, then the Incredible India campaign which saw a global marketing campaign for brand India as an investment destination, and then the celebration of the sixtieth anniversary of India's independence. It was also when the Commonwealth Games came to India, and with it the idea that, you know, India should host the Olympics next. Indian journalism was also influenced by this pride, patriotism and nationalism that was very loud in the air in those years.

In *The Caravan*, our discussion was mostly about the craft and the form of journalism. One line of thinking was, yes, narrative long-form is great, but could we push ourselves to break a scam, influence the narrative, and test the waters with investigative stories? Good long-form non-fiction shall go beyond writing great characters, conflict and drama, and stir up some storms. Magazines like *The New Yorker* and *Esquire* had a tradition of producing great investigative stories. Our investigation into Swami Aseemanand's terrorism activities, the Indian intelligence agencies in Afghanistan, the role of big Indian corporations in pocketing natural resources, the profile on Sathya Sai Baba, and the investigation into the Commonwealth Games kickstarted national and, in some cases, international conversations. The Commonwealth Games scam story for example, published in 2010, was done when we didn't have any staff writers. I tracked down a journalist named Anil Varghese who had left *Tehelka* and was working in a call centre because he was so disappointed with Indian print journalism. I knew he was a good investigative journalist and could do long-form, so I said, 'Why don't you just poke around in the preparations for the upcoming Commonwealth Games?' Just before the Games started, we published our cover story. There were so many scams in it. I remember the investigations editor at *The Times of India* calling me to say, 'Nobody is going to read a 10,000-word story. Are you okay if I just take each of those scams and serialize it with some additional reporting in *The Times of India*?' I said, 'By all means. Please, do.' This was still the quieter phase of *The Caravan*.

We were also experimenting with giving journalists more time to report sensitive stories. Leena Gita Reghunath's landmark investigation into the Hindu terror cases was one such story. She spent two years talking to Swami Aseemanand. She went to the Central Prison in Ambala and interviewed him four times and got him to share the details of the RSS *sarsanghchalak's* role in sanctioning some of the Hindu terror attacks. The story brought Parliament to a standstill.

Long-form journalism is creatively the maximum format for a reporter and writer. Maximum format, because the long-form narrative journalist has the option to write the story with all its complexity, dig deeper, pursue many sources on the subject, get to the best material, and bring to life all the elements of the narrative. The creative attraction to the form and the heady feeling of holding the powerful accountable sticks to the writer like a bug refusing to leave. If the writer is in journalism for social good, and the writer equally likes the creative aspect of storytelling, then narrative journalism is the maximum format. Editorially, this workshopping was taking place in *The Caravan* newsroom in the initial years.

The second phase started with the anti-corruption movement and the rise of Narendra Modi at the national level, all of which threw up great material. By then it was very clear that I could not pursue my original plan to leave the newsroom suddenly. Too many things were happening too quickly in the country.

With the arrival of Modi in Delhi as the rock star of the Hindu right, the stress on Indian media and the judiciary were massive. In our second year we started a media special issue, commissioning long-form stories on major media personalities and institutions. This was something I had wanted to do from my PhD days, to hold a mirror to the media space, as my research was on the sociology of Indian media. In *The New Yorker*, for instance, they used to publish great stories on American media personalities, but in India, we rarely cast a critical eye on the media. Owners, publishers, editors were friends. Many star journalists were lapdogs of the intelligence, supercops, or wealthy businessmen. The composition of newsrooms was even worse. *The Caravan* started covering this space well. By the time the media came under pressure from Modi, who, I think, tamed legacy organizations to be his lapdog, our small newsroom was already publishing critical coverage on the media. But what was new for us since Modi's arrival was the reportage on the judiciary. The stress on the Indian judiciary, and how the top judges and law offices behaved, made for great public-spirited long-form stories.

An investigative story that our newsroom invested heavily on was the mysterious death of Judge Loya, who allegedly refused to take a twelve-million-dollar bribe to acquit Amit Shah. This story saw an unprecedented number of follow-ups, over thirty stories. The material went into the filing of a series of public interest litigations, led to four of the five collegium judges in the Supreme Court holding a press conference, and the Chief Justice of the Supreme Court for the first time in India faced an impeachment process. Such open conversations on the Indian judiciary were only possible because of the diligent and risky work of the The Caravan and a few other journalists.

MK: I wonder if you might say more about the story that I found the most shocking in recent years, that of Judge Loya.[5]

VJ: I remember reading the first draft of the Judge Loya report that found its way to us. I thought it was fiction. The journalist, Niranjan Takle, was a senior reporter working for a prominent magazine. When the magazine he worked for refused to publish the report, he shared it with a bunch of other newsrooms, who also turned it down. In October 2017, an envelope with a printout of four or five pages found its way to us at The Caravan. The story was unbelievable. The cast of characters was big. Judge Loya was

5   Niranjan Takle, 'A Family Breaks Its Silence: Shocking Details Emerge in Death of Judge Presiding over Sohrabuddin Trial', The Caravan, 20 November 2017.

the special CBI judge hearing the case of a fake encounter killing, and the main accused was Amit Shah, the right-hand man of Prime Minister Narendra Modi. Without Amit Shah, there was no Modi, as the world understands him. The political importance of that story was massive. The Supreme Court had shifted the trial out of Gujarat to Maharashtra, and Judge Loya was apparently going to convict Amit Shah, since the evidence was quite solid.

According to Loya's family members, the Chief Justice of the Bombay High Court then offered 100-crore rupees, about twelve million dollars or so, to Judge Loya to acquit Amit Shah. Judge Loya refused the offer. A few days later, the judge died in mysterious circumstances. The government records showed it was a heart attack. We made Niranjan do more reporting, got the testimonies of family members on camera, found more medical records, took the medical reports to independent experts, etc. One story after another, we punctured the government's claims. After Niranjan broke the first two stories, we brought in more reporters, and took the story in all possible directions, showing how Loya's postmortem reports were manipulated, who manipulated them, and so on.

The Caravan stories were met with absolute silence for a few days. The politicians and the government were silent. So were the legacy media houses. After the lull came the plants. To increase believability, these stories appeared in legacy organizations that were not rabidly right-wing like *The Indian Express* and NDTV. Their reports questioned our investigation, and declared that there was nothing suspicious about Judge Loya's death. But we kept at it. Each of our follow-up reports advanced the story step by step. The labour that went in to track every witness who was in the postmortem room, and every employee in the government guest house where Judge Loya stayed, silenced the doubters. The

Supreme Court decided in a hurry to call all Judge Loya death-related PILs from different high courts and passed a verdict that there was no need to investigate Judge Loya's death. Why fear an investigation when the family and friends of Judge Loya had spoken of the bribe offer from the Chief Justice, and when *The Caravan* had systematically produced story after story proving the government claims were wrong? The way the higher offices closed ranks around the Judge Loya story, from the executive to the judiciary to the legacy media, was demonstrative of the times India was going through. In the new phase of authoritarianism, backsliding of democracy, or fascism—whatever it is—everyone was quick to overlook the evidence.

MK: Given the current political scenario in India, with threats to freedom of the press and the aggressive response to any criticism of the state, is there any advice you'd give writers?

VJ: See, in non-fiction journalism, there are different schools, but the school that I like, or I like to position myself close to, is based purely on reportage. Wherever you have facts and information which is verifiable, you have a better chance of public support. Yes, it is true that the tribe of bold publishers is decreasing, and that many do not want to take risks. Having said that, there are newer online platforms that are willing to carry well-reported and critical political journalism. And a story does not need to be published in India to get the attention of Indians. You see a lot of quality political reporting on Indian companies and politicians from outlets like *Financial Times*, *The Guardian*, and the Organized Crime and Corruption Reporting Project.

After Modi came to Delhi, the challenge for a journalist was also about protecting sources. To keep our communications safe and everything under wraps until the story was done. To protect the newsroom from infiltration by intelligence agencies. I felt the pressure at many points, and reminded my colleagues, 'If we are doing investigative long-form journalism, we are not in a newsroom, we are in a war room. We can't afford to make any mistakes.' We have to always ask ourselves, 'What can the consequences be?'

Lastly, one should not self-censor, or accept censorship. If you have facts and are self-censoring, you're censoring the voices of people and the truth they want to see published. If you listen to editors who tell you not to do such stories, and you agree with them, you become part of the well-oiled machinery of compromised media.

My advice is fight your own demons, if they are inside you, like not pursuing a source hard enough, not travelling that extra mile to get some more interesting material, or vanity. Or if the demons are outside you… The demons of censorship outside you are very familiar; they can be in your editor's cabin finding a clever way to argue you away, or in your publisher's office, not giving the reporting expenses that were due, or your immediate superiors who water down your story, or do not display an important story prominently, or delay the publication of a story without any valid reasons, and, even worse, kill the story itself. Faced by such real-life challenges, the journalist's response becomes important. Today's time warrants a lot of courage from the writer. But it is worth living the life of a journalist.

MK: Which, of course, also means working with fact-checkers.

VJ: Indian newsrooms used to have fact-checkers, but with the arrival of computers in the 1980s, fact-checkers were made redundant. When I first moved to Delhi to work in 2001, I did not find any fact-checkers in newsrooms. Editors and copy editors, if they were diligent, caught mistakes. We hired our first fact-checker at *The Caravan* in our second year, I guess. Since then, we continued that tradition. There's no way that an editor or a reporter can overrule a fact-checker. If a fact-checker says something is wrong, there is no way that we can publish it, unless, with fresh evidence, the fact-checker is convinced. I have seen fact-checkers saving many celebrity writers and senior journalists from major embarrassment.

I remember this one instance when a very famous writer in India was giving me a story to publish in *The Caravan*. I said, 'Look, I need the story by so and so date. Besides editing, we need time for fact-checking as well.' The writer was like, 'No, there is no need to fact-check. There is going to be no mistake in the piece.' I didn't want to hurt the writer's ego but I convinced the person to give me the draft early, and as soon as I got the draft, I ran to the fact-checker. I told him, 'Every mistake you find, I'm going to pay you 100 rupees. This writer needs some convincing that fact-checking is vital in the publishing process.' Our fact-checker made a few thousand rupees! There were many factual errors, and the writer was humbled. A few months later, the writer asked me, 'Vinod, can I get your fact-checker for my next book?'

MK: Can you also talk about how you get comments from sources who may be reluctant to speak because they're either afraid or hostile?

VJ: Persistence is vital. In political journalism, sometimes it takes years to get someone to cooperate with you. It took five years for me to convince Mohammad Afzal Guru, the accused in the

Parliament Attack Case, to talk to me. Another example of a source making me wait was a former key official in the finance ministry. In 2011, when I was doing a profile of Manmohan Singh when he was in his prime, the officer refused to talk to me. I would message him once a month—I clocked it on my calendar. I would say, 'Hi, hello sir! How are you doing?' Many days, it was just copy-pasting the same messages. He retired and moved to a small town in India, but was privy to information that nobody had. A few years later, one morning he suddenly responded to my message. It said: 'Take the next flight and come spend the weekend with me.' I sat down with him for two days and nights, and the transcripts were something like 60,000 words. Very rich first-hand material. Deep reporting is like pursuing a person or a thing you are passionate about. Never give up. Be there. Wait till it happens. Always try really, really hard to get the right sources, not *any* source, which is also important at times, but the right sources are vital. There are also people journalists meet in parking lots, elevators, jails, hospital wards, airports and gyms, who can become key players in the development of a story. Sometimes you never know where your right source is. Sometimes, you know exactly who your source is. But that right source gives you the raw material that will make your narrative shine.

RAHUL BHATTACHARYA

INTERVIEWED BY

SAMANTH SUBRAMANIAN

~

'Find your rhythm'

Samanth Subramanian (SS): I've known Rahul for twenty years, and I have realized that he does not talk much about writing. In fact, in all of this time, I think the only serious thing he has told me about his writing is that he started writing with pencils. This is the only information he will divulge about his process, so this is an opportunity for me to ask a lot of questions. Let me start by asking, what are you reading now?

Rahul Bhattacharya (RB): At this moment I'm reading *The Collected Tales of Nikolai Gogol*; he's such a funny writer, maybe the funniest I have ever read. I read *Dead Souls*, his great novel, a little while ago, and his stories are what I'm reading, as well as dipping into a few other story collections—there's a Kafka collection I've been diving in and out of as well as one by George Saunders.

SS: Are you looking at short stories for something in particular?

RB: No, it has actually never occurred to me to write short stories, and I don't think I'd be any good either. There's so much you can learn from a short story, just in the way that one can learn much from poetry or music. Just because they are more compressed forms, I think it's easier to write an excellent short story, or almost the perfect short story. Novels are almost always failures, even the best novels are just honourable failures. There's so much to negotiate, so I like being able to dip into something that is perfect. Some of these stories are so compressed, they're heart-breaking in a way that novels can't be, or, they can be moving in a vivid way that novels can't be. Novels are what I like reading most, and it is the form that I am most attracted to. I don't read short stories with the view to write [them], just with the view to read.

SS: So, it's kind of almost a counterintuitive thing—the received knowledge about these two forms. The short story is always harder to do, because it has less space in which to achieve this perfection that you're talking about, and to hit all the high points that you want out of fiction. Whereas a novel allows space for mistakes and to come back on track. The short story is the T20 game, and the novel is the Test match, is the way I have always thought of it.

RB: That's not an analogy I would go with. T20 almost fundamentally changes the rules of the game. I mean the basic rules are all the same, but I don't think you can get the best of cricket in T20, you can get a lot of it. But in a short story you can get the finest, the highest calibre of writing. It's just that because you're working in a tighter space, there's more control. Your story usually has shorter arcs to cover, unless you're writing 'Brokeback Mountain', which is basically an epic in a short story, as the movie showed you—the scale and the canvas of the film—but it's a tight short story.

Think about Edna O'Brien's short story 'The Rug', which is a heart-breaking, beautiful story narrated by a young Irish girl. O'Brien has such a beautiful narrative voice, it's poetic, it's innocent as well as knowing, sometimes. It's about this family who are a little hard up. The father is a bit of a friendly wastrel, and the mother is always slogging for every little thing they get. It's been their dream to cover up the linoleum floor with a carpet.

One day in the post, they receive a magnificent rug, and they don't know who sent it, and they think, 'Who sent this? Could it be somebody from America? Who could it be?' Just the description of the young girl watching her mother and what this means to her is so beautifully done. I won't tell you what happened, but in about seven or eight pages, there's so much in there. T20 can't do that.

SS: Edna O'Brien's voice is sort of funny and knowing, and one of the striking things about your writing is that there is a very strong sense of voice. I think, although maybe you disagree, that you came by this quite early. Even when you were doing magazine writing in the early 2000s for the cricket monthly *Wisden Asia Cricket*, where you used to write profiles of cricketers, even then I seem to remember that same kind of voice. It's usually very hard to describe voice, but I tried to figure out the adjectives that would fit yours, and I came up with 'wry and slightly detached', 'curious', 'really alive to the sensory aspects of the world that you're describing', and 'very rhythmic'. I'm curious to know what your thinking is about how one comes by voice.

RB: It's a difficult question. I think there are writers who find their voice, and it kind of stays with them, and they perfect it. I'm not sure I would fall into that category. I feel the first voice I hit on as a cricket writer was a natural voice—it just came to me. It was a voice without self-consciousness, because I hadn't planned on being a cricket writer or writer or journalist at all. In some ways, I must be a very unqualified person to talk about writing and literature, because it's something that happened by accident. I realized how much I liked it by actually doing it.

My first book was a cricketing travelogue with the Indian cricket team to Pakistan called *Pundits from Pakistan* (Picador, 2005). I was trained for that, because I did cricket reporting for two or three years, straight out of my graduation in pure mathematics. But everything after that, every piece, the second book, the third—which has been going on forever, hopefully I finish it sometime soon—has been a struggle to find that voice, to see which voice would fit this project.

You're right, in the sense that I'm sure there will be many commonalities in this voice. I don't even know how one finds it, like you can't change your speaking voice to a degree, you just have it, and it is what it is. So, with your writing voice, you can control it to an extent, you can guide it in certain directions and, as your writing ambitions grow, you can change it to fit moods, characters, situations. It's part of the writing technique that you practice while reading and writing. But I think there is something fundamental to your writing voice, like your speaking voice, or height, or hair growth, that just is and you work with that.

One important thing is not to work against that. I made this mistake very many times in drafts, and perhaps even in published stuff—to go against your natural voice can be a big mistake. To write with greater gravitas than the writing merits, or to try to be funny or slapstick, when you just don't have the talent for it. I think the easier thing to do is to save your voice from becoming something that it can't be. The struggle to actually *find* your voice is like a discovery. I don't even know how one goes about that.

SS: You're right in the sense that it tends to vary from project to project, and very often the voice, I think, is dictated by the material. Even the things you said now—for example, sometimes you feel like you need to impart more gravitas to a piece of writing.

That feeling actually comes from the material, it doesn't come from anything else. I'm surprised to hear you say that your voice is changing, or does change. But maybe I only see, as you say, the common threads that have remained over the twenty years.

RB: I'm too close to it, maybe a little more sensitive to things that may not actually be big changes. In my novel *The Sly Company of People Who Care* (Picador, 2012), for example, the voice was dictated totally by material, since I was in the Caribbean. I don't naturally go around speaking or writing in the Caribbean inflection, or didn't till I spent time there. I felt that in the language of the Caribbean, the Patois, there was so much life, energy, all kinds of vividness. There were compressed histories in some of those words and how they came about through the interaction of languages and cultures. I felt that I must find a way to reintegrate this, to an extent, in my narrative voice. When I came back, that voice was in my head all the time and the challenge was, 'How do I marry these two things—the very raw Patois which was in my head with some kind of literary narrative voice?'

SS: It was such a bold exercise. Was it something you thought consciously about all the time while crafting the book? And, related to this, I'm curious about the stage of a project at which your voice first comes in? Is your first draft all voice and you then refine it? Or is voice something that is layered onto a project draft after draft until it acquires this sheen of final-ness?

RB: In *Sly Company* the voice came very early. I don't mean the voice came to me instantly, but it came because I came back with so much of the voice in my head. In fact, our common editor and agent, Shruti [Debi], had told me, 'You need to make this a little

more intelligible. It's too much in your own head.' The challenge
was to start detaching myself a little bit from it. Being able to write
the opening paragraphs in the opening chapter was very crucial
to how the book played out. Looking back, a lot went into the
sort of linguistic energy involved, and what that recreation means
and what that can do.

That's why I think my voice is changing because the second
novel has not developed in that way at all; it's coming from a totally
different place and its development has been totally different. That
said, I think there are things about voice that one falls back on,
rhythm being one of them. The few things I thought about start
obviously at the level of expression, at words and phrases, and
just the precision—the economy of the well-chosen word, some
kind of attention to vocabulary, a battle against staleness, or the
war against cliché. You can't only be relying on things that have
been written, because that almost implies the world has stopped,
like life and thoughts and emotions have paused, because you
are up against this paucity of words and expressions to describe
something new. It starts at that level, right? 'Okay, what am I really
describing? Let me not rely on borrowed phrases and words, and
ways of saying things.' From there, what's very important to me is
pacing, just the idea of being able to generate a certain momentum
in your work, momentum which is well-judged. Sometimes you
need to bring a feeling of exhilaration, or it could be something
more pensive or contemplative or whatever it is. But being alive
to pacing, I think, is very important to writing.

SS: And by pacing you also mean sometimes you slow things
down and sometimes you speed things up? There's a kind of shift
happening.

RB: Definitely. I think very few writers can pull off constant fast momentum all the time—that kind of relentless energy. Some writers can, but it's hard, and I think even they would pause at the right moment. At the same time, I think I'm broadly for keeping things moving. You have someone like [Albert] Camus in *The Outsider* and that's a brilliant novel, but it's seventy-six pages long. You do too much of stasis and ennui, and things like that, over 400 pages, your readers will slit their wrists. I like keeping things going, unless I have something to slow down for and think hard about.

Once you get your pacing right, then you develop rhythm. You come to rhythm when you've got sentences stacking up one upon the other. Sentences which may not be quote-worthy in themselves though they might be excellent sentences producing note upon note of this kind of miraculous effect of energy, and you're feeling things in your heart when you are reading—you're singing or you're feeling sad, it's touching you. That rhythm is hard to get. It's of course something that you have to rehearse and work on, but sometimes even in your raw draft, you see that happening; hitting that kind of rhythm. That rhythm is something that I aspire for, to read and to write. And tied in with that is timing—what comes in at what time, what goes in at what time.

If you stay with the music analogy, I think my rhythms are perhaps dictated by music. I'm a great admirer of musicians and performing artists, and all the work that goes in for them to achieve what they do. There's a great South African song called 'Pata Pata' by Miriam Makeba that's more than fifty years old. If you hear that version, and you hear other African versions of it, it has a very, very sweet, full, juicy, beautiful African sound. This song has been covered thousands of times by thousands of artists. If you hear the Jamaicans do it, if you hear The Skatalites—which is like a ska jazz band—they have this almost militant insistence, an energy, horns coming in one after the other. Jamaicans are very, very tight musicians, very disciplined and that has its own hypnosis. Then there's a Puerto Rican orchestra called El Gran Combo de Puerto Rico, and their version has this spectacular horn refrain which is like a wild shriek—I think it's a trumpet or maybe a tenor sax, I don't know—and it comes in and goes out; it just reimagines this thing entirely. All of these great musicians know exactly when to drop something and when to come out, and what works perfectly with their rhythm and arrangement. A lot of writing is like that. That wild shriek of the trumpet is not something people would have imagined in 'Pata Pata' but it works so well.

SS: Let me press you a little bit on this rhythm thing because I'm really curious about it. It sounds good when we say that writing is rhythmic, and maybe one aspect to this is if we read writing out aloud, there is a beat to the sentences in terms of how long they are. Let's say length is one aspect of it—how you alternate short and long sentences is one feature of rhythm. From a writing perspective, what else is a feature of rhythm when you say, for example, when to come in and when to step out?

RB: There's a bit from Toni Morrison in *Jazz* that has an obvious music connotation. This is an astonishing novel, just the way she pulls it together. The basic story is that this older married man takes a young lover, then he shoots her dead, and there's a funeral. This is all happening right at the start. The wife of this man goes to disfigure the corpse of the young girl who had been in an affair with her husband. From there Morrison takes you into the lives of these three people, back into their stories, and she uses very strange narrative techniques. The narrators are slightly on the outside, but speak with an intimate 'I' voice. Maybe there's more than one of them.

In the early part of the book she's describing this journey from the country into the city of freed people—former slaves, going to the city to make their lives. The whole thing spreads to about 20–30 pages where she's constantly coming back to the city and narrating its appeal. It starts with this great first-person 'I'm crazy about this city', which is really colloquial, but declarative. The next sentence is 'Daylight slants like a razor cutting the buildings in half.' Then two chapters later, we are coming back to the journey of these protagonists in the early twentieth century into the city that gives a sense of Morrison's very elliptical style—she keeps coming back to things, back to similar images, sometimes similar words, but she kind of keeps it going. It's extraordinary.

She does this, like I said, over pages and pages. She has these stunning images in between of the city, sometimes almost too many of them, like little frames of sights and sounds, and it almost gets tiresome, but then you tell yourself not all of these images will stay with everybody, but what does will hit you so hard, it will be a part of your own life like you've seen it.

Morrison's rhythm is of a particular kind, whereas Gogol is different. His rhythm is very propulsive, always forward; he's not elliptical, he's not giving you these short, tight, poetic images; he is relentlessly funny. He's very descriptive, even with nature. But his rhythm—it's very unusual to see a writer with this energy, this unafraid to be constantly funny and keep things constantly moving from sentence to sentence. Another great comic novel, which is so different from Gogol in every respect except the satirical eye, is [V.S. Naipaul's] *A House for Mr Biswas*, where he has simple short sentences but each of them is moving things along. Overt contemplation in the novel is very small. A great piece of writing is when a writer has found their rhythm, and their way to deal with the material.

SS: That's really good. We also talked about doing something similar with a non-fiction piece. Do you have one that you want to share?

RB: I thought about a piece of writing I had received as an editor at *The Cricket Monthly*, which is the long-form arm of ESPNcricinfo. com. It was by the brilliant Australian writer Christian Ryan on Dennis Lillee, the great Australian fast bowler of the 1970s and early 1980s. The piece is called 'The Thirty-Ninth Summer of DK Lillee'. It's the most extraordinary and unusual piece of sports writing I think you'll ever read. Four or so years after he retired, Lillee decides to make a comeback because he just can't give it up, and wants another taste of it. He warms up in Australia, and goes to the county season in England. Christian chronicles this small chapter in his life with such vividness, attention to detail and gusto. The story of the great *The New Yorker* reporter Joseph Mitchell also runs through the text. Suddenly, Mitchell will come in, and then Lillee will come back, he'll go out, Mitchell will come back in. The common thread being that Mitchell, for the last thirty or so years of his life, kept going into the *The New Yorker* office after he had retired. They gave him an office because he was such a great reporter for them. He kept working noiselessly, or sometimes they heard typing, working on a piece that he never submitted, on a character called Joe Gould who was apparently writing the oral history of the world which again was a work that never really existed. But Mitchell just kept going into the office. So, it was the idea of perfection, the idea of not giving up your craft, and just having more of it. It's just layered in the most brilliant way.

Can I ask you a question on this rhythm in non-fiction? One of the remarkable non-fiction pieces I read recently was your report from Sri Lanka on going back to trace the lives of two rich, young bombers[6] who blew themselves up—who knows why—to create one of the great tragedies of post-war Sri Lanka. It starts with a great scene of the potential bomber having this moment of hesitation just before he presses the button. Then there's the detonation. People are confused; somebody thinks chandeliers have fallen on the floor, somebody else thinks there's a fire, and there's an incredible detail of a man identifying it as being a suicide bombing because he has seen a decapitated head. From Sri Lanka's history of suicide bombers, they know that's what happens when somebody straps themselves with explosives and blows themselves up; the head separates.

It starts with that and from this point you take us to the father of these bombers, then you take us to each of these sons, from there you come down to the recruiter—a very charismatic man who can talk for hours and convince anybody of anything—and from there to this rabble-rousing creature who's perhaps the mastermind, finishing with the bomber at the site of detonation, leaving us pretty much exactly where we started, except everything's changed in your understanding of this, all that's gone on to this ghastly event. But also at the same time, honouring what we don't know, honouring the fact that there's a mystery to this, that we never know why somebody does this. I wanted to ask you about that

---

6   Samanth Subramaniam, 'Two Wealthy Sri Lankan Brothers Become Suicide Bombers. But Why?', *The New York Times Magazine*, 2 July 2020.

structure. Is that something that suggested itself while reporting, or is that something that you sat back and said, 'This is how I will map my story?' I don't know whether you map stories at all. I usually don't unless I'm stuck somewhere and untangle things.

SS: I was going to ask you that at some point. I map stories all the time these days. The first two books that I wrote, I didn't map at all. Then, about six years ago, I found that very often with reporting non-fiction pieces, there is so much material, that I can't afford to wing it. So, I now have a page-long structure on a legal pad next to me, broken up into the sections of the piece. At some point, I end up counting for almost every paragraph in the final piece. Everything is mapped out in the initial structure, or at least the function of what a particular paragraph is.

RB: When do you make this diagram or flowchart?

SS: After all my reporting but before I have started writing. Of course, it's flexible. The structure you described right now is, in one sense, the easiest structure. It starts *in medias res*—it's the most dramatic action I'm going to describe in the entire piece, so why would I not lead with that, which is a man blowing himself up? And then you go back and go chronologically until you come back to his present, his last moment, so to speak. Let's move on. How do you develop awareness as you read? And, I'm curious about how you read? Are you reading with a writer's hat on, looking for ways in which a piece of prose works or are you reading with the reader's hat on?

RB: I almost never read with the writer's hat on deliberately. It may be happening subliminally, because I like writing to hit me in a way that I can't actually identify what it is. I am just absorbed. It's like you absorb when you walk through streets and you're picking things up. You don't know what it is exactly, but things are catching your eye all the time. But unless you're going out with a specific project, if you go with a very limited agenda, you will perhaps not even be successful, it may not be that much fun. Since I started writing professionally, I'm sure that I read with more awareness than I would have earlier, but it's never ever deliberate.

SS: Also, as you get an idea for a project, do you also get the idea for the music and the rhythm right away, or does it develop as the project goes along?

RB: The first two books suggested themselves very strongly to me. This third one is a more complex book, so I don't know whether the idea of a single spark is always true, and always true for every writer. I know there are writers who start with one image and like building outwards. There are writers who are also coming from a very holistic view like, 'This is what I want to do with this project', and then you narrow it down. I think there have to be sparks for me. Without being genuinely interested in an idea, and being really curious about it, you can't really go to an excellent place with it. You can do functional jobs, and we have to do functional writing sometimes as well.

SS: If you're writing a non-fiction piece about something that could be considered a niche interest, how do you approach it? Your piece on Mary Kom,[7] the boxer, comes to mind. It was published in a magazine that used to be called *Intelligent Life*, which is now called *1843*, and it's a British magazine, so readers don't necessarily know Mary Kom and they definitely don't know the status she occupies in India. So how do you bridge the gap between a reader who's not quite as aware and has your sky-high level of enthusiasm about the subject?

RB: If you're writing a piece of non-fiction, you are almost beholden to lay things out a bit. What I sometimes can't stand— sorry to take such a harsh view of this—in reading about our own societies in foreign publications, is the constant annotation and explaining the most basic terms. That can be very tedious to read, and it's partly because of the formulaic manner in which these things are done. I think it is our duty to explain to those innocent about what we may think are very obvious details, we have that kind of responsibility. But it is great when we can do that through characters, or through other means. Lively writing does that work. Writing well and with attention and some kind of vigour. It's probably how you'll enjoy writing the most as well. I mean it's not always easy to do. You're always facing your own limitations of knowledge, of energy, of your ability to pull off something the way you want to, but the only way it will be interesting for yourself is if you're writing with that kind of attention towards something.

---

7   Rahul Bhattacharya, 'The Phenomenal Mary Kom', *The Economist*, 6 August 2012.

JAMIL JAN KOCHAI

INTERVIEWED BY

KARAN MAHAJAN

❧

'What is your novel saying in the midst of the larger conversation?'

Karan Mahajan (KM): Jamil Jan Kochai is one of the most astonishing talents working in American literature today. I was blown away when I read his first book, *99 Nights in Logar* (Bloomsbury, 2019), which effortlessly combines the voice of a pious Afghan-American Muslim with rebellious Sac-town slang. His new collection, *The Haunting of Hajji Hotak and Other Stories* (Viking, 2022) takes that project one step further, infusing his storytelling with formal experimentation and a furious magic realism that reminds me of Gogol or of Kafka. This is the world where you'll meet weeping goats, praying monkeys and, of course, Pashtun fuckboys. Like Salman Rushdie and Hanif Kureishi, Jamil takes supposedly clashing markers of identity and throws them into generous and surprising conversation.

Jamil, you said in an interview, 'The term Afghan-American itself disturbed me. Rather than being a pontification, the hyphen seemed to reveal a chasm, a rupture inside of which rested all the violence and contradictions of the American War.' I'm curious about how you went from that point of feeling a deep rupture to writing with an acceptance of hybridity.

Jamil Jan Kochai (JJK): Fiction allows me the space to explore the contradictions occurring throughout my life and the way they impacted how I saw myself, how I saw history, and, in particular, how I saw the relationship between the United States and Afghanistan, who, for much of my life, were at war. That was something that I found very difficult to contend with for a long

245

time—how one can belong to both these places while these places are actively at war. But fiction allows for contradiction. When you think about magical realism, for example, the term seems contradictory, but then you read magical realist texts and they feel like the most honest, most truthful and most beautiful way to tell a story—at least for me.

KM: Can you talk about the evolution of your influences?

JJK: When I first started writing fiction seriously, I had begun to conceptualize what literature—with a capital L—was. I thought it was largely rooted in older texts by white men. Writers like Cormac McCarthy, Ernest Hemingway, William Faulkner, James Joyce, a bunch of dead white guys, essentially. There's nothing wrong with being influenced by these writers—they are deeply important to this day to me—but what ended up happening was that I wrote exactly like those white writers, and my stories sounded terrible. McCarthy, in particular, was deeply influential, and so I would write stories about Afghan teenagers in Sacramento, but in the voice of McCarthy, a kind of neo-Biblical prose, and it was very bad.

  It wasn't until I started graduate school and began reading Sandra Cisneros and Junot Díaz and Denis Johnson and George Saunders that things changed. I was introduced to Saunders and Díaz at the same time—two fantastic short-story writers who were very popular when I started graduate school—and the thing about both of these writers is that they write in a style of voice that's very natural and organic. It's not pretentious or overly sophisticated like you'd see in McCarthy or Joyce or Faulkner, but it made me realize that I could write a story in the more laid-back, down to earth, natural and multilingual voice that I had grown up with. That really opened up a fictional space for my voice.

KM: You've talked about how reading *The Thousand and One Nights* and channeling your parents' oral storytelling was influential, but I'm wondering about the flipside. Did you—like many South Asian writers—feel hemmed in by duty? Did it take a while to reach a point of being irresponsible and playful?

JJK: I did often feel hemmed in by anxieties regarding what my family or my community might think of my writing, and at times it was a little debilitating. But with this story collection in particular, I tried to allow myself as much freedom as possible to write as closely to the characters as I could. So, whether it's the college students in 'Hungry Ricky Daddy', or the perspective of two middle-aged doctors in 'Return to Sender', or an older Afghan mother in 'Enough', it was important that I got as close to their perspective, to their voice as possible, without hemming myself in too much with this tendency towards piety, which I think is often present in my work.

KM: That's a great answer. I have a question which basically consists of two words, 'kite' and 'runner'. You've talked about how *The Kite Runner*, inadvertently, was a fillip for you to get going with your novel. Could you describe that?

JJK: Growing up in the States, anytime I told anyone that I was Afghan, and if they knew that I was studying literature, they would ask me if I read *The Kite Runner*, and I'd tell them in a disappointed way that I had. I read the book for the first time when I was about fifteen years old at a period in my life when I was opening myself up to novels and books. I was immensely disappointed, not just by the story itself—I have issues with the development of the story, the way the author depicts Afghanistan, the different sorts of political and ideological things he's doing in the text regarding what he decides to leave in historically and what he leaves out—but my main issue was the prose. I thought the writing was very bad. At that time, I was also reading Toni Morrison and Gabriel García Márquez, immensely talented prose stylists whose sentences would make you lose your breath and then I read this Afghan guy whose writing was so choppy and plain, it was difficult to get through the book. *The Kite Runner* was so deeply disappointing it became oddly inspirational because I ended up closing that book and thinking that even I could do better.

KM: As you and I both know, America is a very large and insular country. That said, more than twenty years have passed since *The Kite Runner* came out and I'm curious about how your work has been received, especially in the US. What about this response has interested you? What has surprised you? What has upset you?

JJK: It's largely been very positive. I was anticipating, especially with *99 Nights in Logar*, that there would be backlash. The book is anti-war, anti-US military. I was expecting some pushback, and that didn't end up happening. The pushback that I got was with the use of Pashto in the novel, which a lot of people had issues with.

The second book got a review in *The New York Times* that was not very flattering. Basically, it was by a white veteran who had written a book on Afghanistan. He seemed to have issues with how I was depicting the white characters in my book, with how I was depicting the military and the war in Afghanistan as a whole. For me, that was the first time that I felt—especially from someone in a position of power—that there was significant political resistance to what I was trying to accomplish.

KM: I know that review in *The New York Times* was deeply disappointing, but also a useful piece of information about how a certain kind of white person reads literature. The reviewer had based the review on what he thought was a depiction of one white character who appears on one page, but it was just fascinating as it confirmed a suspicion one has about such readers; it's not true of all white readers, obviously. There's a lack of self-awareness in America about the role the US played in Afghanistan, and you've done a wonderful job in your essays and stories in pushing back against that.

Another thing I wanted to come back to was something you touched upon a little bit, of being in graduate school and discovering writers like Saunders, Cisneros and Díaz, and I was wondering if you can talk about what the environment of the writing workshop has been like for you? And, whether you would encourage it for other writers?

JJK: The writing workshop can be dangerous for writers who are writing experimental work. Oftentimes, it can be very difficult for workshop writers to wrap their heads around it, and there can be a need to fix it, to strip it away of everything that makes the writing special and unique, brave and frightening. That being said, the writing workshop was very important for me in my development as a writer. You've heard a lot of horror stories about the workshop, with writers coming into workshops and hearing racist things, sexist things, or their work being attacked—I think sometimes it's even worse when it's not attacked and the writers are just, very sincerely, stripping the story apart of everything that makes it beautiful. At the same time, I think there are also a lot of different spaces in which you'll go in and end up coming out a better writer, especially if you're careful about who you intend to study with. One of the most important things that happened for me when I was in a workshop was that my instructor at the time told us that we only want to take away 10 per cent of what we hear. That raised the alarm for me. I learned to take in commentary and critique that were aligned with what I was trying to accomplish and not to reshape my work to appease another writer.

KM: I know you're not in a workshop at the moment, so I wonder what your editing process is like. How do you maintain a balance between the longer stories—which I love—like 'Hungry Ricky Daddy' or 'The Tale of Dully's Reversion', their wildness and sprawl—and the concision that is necessary in the structure of a short story?

JJK: For almost thirteen years straight I've been in one workshop or another almost every single year. I depended upon the workshop for a structural form: the deadlines were very helpful for me; there was always a ready group of outside eyes that I could work off of; and then, of course, there was always a mentor that I could have a final check with, 'Is this actually working, professor? Tell me! Accept me!'

Now that I've left the workshop model behind, it's been difficult, but I've also attuned myself more to self-editing, to figuring out what I really want for my stories, the limitations, etc. I have a number of close readers that I'll show my work to. I also have a pretty good relationship with my agent—she has a spectacular eye for figuring out when a short story works. That's been my state of mind right now, just taking everything that I've picked up along the way and developing my ability to excel at it.

KM: There's obviously the workshop of your peers, but there's also your family, right? I'm curious: what is the relationship between you, your work, your parents and your siblings? How do you write stories knowing that they will be consumed not just by strangers like us but by family members?

JJK: I've tried to keep my family as involved as possible, especially when I'm directly drawing from their experiences. I send almost all of my stories to my siblings first, and I've been really fortunate and really blessed that my siblings—they're all younger than me—are well read and understand what I'm trying to accomplish. They've developed a great critical eye for characterization, in particular, and it's one of those things where, if anything, the main comments I'll get will be, 'I don't think you depicted this character badly enough', and so on.

But ultimately, I feel it is my duty as a writer and an artist to depict my stories as honestly and as truthfully as I can manage, and if that means upsetting some people then so be it. I need to make sure that I don't—for lack of a better term—become frightened of what the story demands.

KM: Another thing that I find fascinating about you as a writer is that you are adamant that you want to live in Sacramento, where you grew up. Can you talk a little bit more about the relationship between the writer and place? And also whether Logar will continue to play the central role it has played in your mind, or if you're moving away from that?

JJK: When I first started writing fiction, it was almost all about Logar; for me Sacramento wasn't an interesting topic. I think part of that had to do with the fact that the first stories I ever heard were about Logar—the stories that my parents told me, that my grandparents told me. In a lot of ways, the starting point of my literary or storytelling imagination revolved around Logar. I don't think that's something that I'll ever be able to escape. I'm going to be writing about Logar for the rest of my life.

But I will say that when I moved away from Sacramento for the first time, I immediately felt an impulse to begin writing about Sacramento. Funnily enough, there was something about leaving that place behind and feeling torn away from it—Sacramento being the place where most of the people I love are living—made me feel, 'I've got to write about Sacramento.' Since then my relationship with Sacramento has only become more complicated and layered. I went through this period where I was doing historical research on Logar; reading books about the war and the agriculture, the geology and plant and animal life, and now I'm doing that same thing with Sacramento. I'm trying to rediscover and relearn the place that I grew up in. My work is very, I would say, location centred.

For a long time I thought of Sacramento as an uninteresting place. Now that I've thought more and more about it, it becomes more and more strange, it becomes more and more surreal, it becomes, funny enough, more and more violent. The more I'm re-conceptualizing how I think about violence—for so long I thought violence was a war, I thought of violence as a soldier shooting a civilian—I've come to learn that that is only one form of violence. What I'm thinking about more, with how I'm writing about Sacramento, is structural violence—the ways that violence can be written into the structure of a city, the way a highway is paved, the ways that neighbourhoods are segregated, the way a police state is built, the threat of violent imprisonment, and how it all comes together to create an eerie, non-violent kind of violence.

KM: Such a superb answer. I want to ask you about the novel you're working on right now. Is the process of writing and thinking through this novel quite different from the previous two books?

JJK: One of things that I loved about writing the short-story collection was that it wasn't as obsessive and as anxiety-inducing as the novel had been. With the novel, I felt I was constantly inside the world of the novel. I would wake up thinking about the novel; I'd spend my day thinking about the novel; I'd go to sleep at night thinking about the novel; and everything revolved around the novel. With the short story collection, I felt much more freedom to be able to put the stories away, or to put one story away and think about another, and to play around with form, voice and language. It didn't feel like the stakes were as immense as with the novel.

Now that I'm working on the second novel, I've kind of prepared myself, but I do find myself falling back into that obsessive nature. When I went to sleep last night, the last thing I thought about was the novel, and when I woke up this morning, the first thing I thought about was the novel. I'm trying to figure out new ways to think about how to construct the novel. I wish my office were open. I have poster boards all over my wall of different things that I'm mapping out. I drew a sketch of the location of the novel, I have character sketches. I'm thinking over and over again of how to figure out the novel's true form.

KM: I'd rather not be reminded of my own anxieties! What recommendations do you have for self-editing, especially for a second draft? What do you look for in your first readers?

JJK: My natural instinct is to be very brutal with my writing, but in the early stages I'm constantly reminding myself, 'Go easy. You're going to be able to figure it out. Allow space for play, allow space for experimentation, allow space to mess up.' I think it's really important to be comfortable with the idea of bad writing initially, or writing that doesn't make sense, or a plot line that feels overdone. But in the secondary stages, and especially once you've got a manuscript that you're pretty happy with, it's important to start getting honest with yourself, and to be as brutal as you can with what you're trying to accomplish with the writing.

One of the things I do for myself is to figure out the place of my work within the larger conversation of what my work is trying to accomplish. So, if you're settled on the idea that your work is about war, or migration, or identity—I'm sort of listing the different topics that I'm constantly engaging with in my work— then it's important to venture outward and figure out—especially in contemporary writing—what other novels are out there that are like the one that you're writing. There's always, I think, going to be other work—no matter how fresh your work is—that's mirroring your work in one way or another. I think it's pivotal to figure out what your novel is saying in the midst of the larger conversation. It also provides you with a different framework in terms of the critical eye and of what you're doing.

I continue to be quite proud of my first novel, *99 Nights in Logar*, but looking back now, I wish I had a larger sense of what my work was doing, inside the conversation regarding immigrant literature, in particular. If I had thought about it, *99 Nights in Logar* would be a different book, and in many ways, a better book, a more complicated one.

KM: While weaving history in fiction, how does one decide which aspects of history contribute to the storytelling, and which aspects become exposition?

JJK: With *99 Nights*, certain elements of the history of Afghanistan were crucial to the development of the story, to understanding characters, but I kept facing the question of 'How do I introduce this history without it becoming too expositional? Without it slowing down the story?' I have to prioritize the story, so if historical knowledge is going to take away from the story, I find a different method. You can have other characters tell the stories within the story, right? So, in that way, instead of trying to force this textual history into the story itself, you can turn a country's history into an oral history, and that's one of the things that I did with *99 Nights*.

The other thing is to be playful with it. When I was at the University of California, Davis, Zadie Smith came to visit, and one of the things that she said—we were talking about style in writing—was that style comes down to the way that a writer navigates time in their story. At the time, I was thinking, 'Well, that's not true. There's narrative voice and sentence structure, and diction; there's all these different things.' But the more I write, and the more I think back on that comment, the more I am convinced that everything does come down to time. It's about understanding where you need to slow down, where you need to speed up, and where you need to go backwards or forwards in time. There are different methods; you can have a character, have particular items or locations that evoke memories, but the main thing I'm trying to emphasize here is to be as creative and as playful as possible.

KM: What were you reading while you were writing the stories in *The Haunting of Hajji Hotak*? Were there certain books you were purposely trying not to read?

JJK: Oh, that's a great question! I was trying to avoid novels! I didn't want to go back into that headspace, because I was writing a story collection and was afraid that I might get a novel idea in the middle of the story collection, and that I would abandon the stories in order to write a novel. I was reading a lot of story collections that I had really come to depend upon. *Drown* by Junot Díaz, *Woman Hollering Creek and Other Stories* by Sandra Cisneros, Daniyal Mueenuddin's *In Other Rooms, Other Wonders*. I was reading a lot of history, a lot of philosophy, but the one type of book that I was avoiding at all costs was novels, in particular, those big, fat novels that suck you in and take over your life.

PARUL SEHGAL

INTERVIEWED BY

ISAAC CHOTINER

~

'My idea of the reader is
somebody who has better
things to do'

Isaac Chotiner (IC): Mark Twain said that no man is under oath at a funeral oration, but I think that's also true when you're talking about colleagues. In this case, I don't have to say anything untrue; Parul is an amazing friend, colleague and writer. Would you like to talk a little bit about your early life and background, and how you got into journalism?

Parul Sehgal (PS): Thank you, Isaac. My background is haphazard, and like a cautionary tale, I fear. I grew up in the States, India, the Philippines and Hungary, and travelled a lot growing up; we moved every three years. I'd always been a demon reader, that's the one thing I knew, but I didn't know how to translate that into any form of gainful employment. Growing up, I wanted to do something with writing, but I wasn't sure what. I dabbled in film-making and playwriting. I thought about writing a novel. I was living in India when I heard about MFA programmes in the States. I was so unmoored at that time and it seemed so appealing.

I came to Columbia University and studied, of all things, fiction writing, which I had no aptitude for at all—I had a great aptitude for fiction reading which I learned does *not* translate—but I realized how much I liked the work of criticism. It seemed to come to me more naturally, all the nosy discussions around fiction. What does this book mean? Where does it come from? What sort of reception does it receive? What goes into the reception? What are the values we associate with fiction? What are our criteria? Where do *they* come from? All of that I found fascinating, and once I finished the programme, I started freelancing. I got staff jobs editing here and there, one magazine or another, moved to National Public Radio, and then *The New York Times*. And, always on the side, I kept up this pace of trying to write about books— wherever they would have me—short pieces, long pieces, profiles. I was trying to cast my voice and write for as many different places and platforms as I could. It felt very important to see how I could maintain something of my own voice while slipping into one style or another, or one format or another. I was very dogged. The job of a literary critic opened up with *The Times*, and I started to do that professionally. I moved over to *The New Yorker* in 2021.

IC: You said you were 'a demon reader'. Does that mean more than reading a lot or reading quickly?

PS: Both. I wanted to swallow the library. I felt shame about what I hadn't read; I charted my own education. It helped that I had a great contempt for education in general, and teachers, and going to school and all of that. I disliked all of it while being fairly good at it—which was confusing. I always thought 'I can do it myself', and, I think, that's where some of the demon reading, the autodidactism, comes into being.

IC: What do you think it was about criticism that spoke to you early on? Were there certain critics, or was there something about the form?

PS: It's a good question. I think it was first the form. It was newspaper reviews that turned on the light in me. There's a tone in the criticism that I really responded to then, as now. It wasn't didactic. It wasn't self-entranced and it didn't usually want to teach you anything. It wanted to level with you, it wanted to tell you if the book was worth your time, your money, your attention. It was on the reader's side—conspiratorial. The critic thinks about the reader's pleasure, they want the books to be equal to the reader and I found that way of thinking about books and writing, about culture, enthralling.

IC: I was reading an old interview of yours where you said, '… because criticism is performative, the reader is implicitly included', which suggests a little bit of something that you said now. Do you think that's more true of criticism than other forms of writing?

PS: It's certainly more true of novel writing and essay writing, in which you can create something involute—sort of like a seashell. You can create something for yourself and the reader is invited. But criticism, for me, always includes components of performance. At the base level, my writing provides a service. I want to tell the reader: 'Is this book worth reading? How do we think about this writer? What's going on with their career? Where does this book fit in with what they've done? Where does it fit in with other things that are happening right now?' But the criticism I love to read and strive to write also provides its own aesthetic experience for the reader; it is conscious of its own demands on the reader's time and attention.

IC: You mentioned earlier about wanting to inform the reader in some way and, I think, some critics—I wouldn't want to divide them into two categories—would say that what they truly love is to tell the reader about what is wonderful out there, what books

are wonderful, what novels they should be reading, not of some
ethical sense but because they will truly bring you joy and learning.
And some critics want to warn the reader about bad things out
there, whether they are bad political opinions, or bad prose, to
stand guard over what they hold dear and make sure that people
know what isn't good. Do you feel like either of those ideas spoke
to you in some way? Or, is that dichotomy too clean?

PS: I think that dichotomy is fine and applies to a lot of critics.
There's a sort of hygienic function associated with criticism—
critics who appoint themselves to keep the literary ecosystem
clean and standards high. But I can get so much out of a bad
book. The book I'm reviewing now is not particularly good, but
thinking about it is so interesting. Its flaws are so interesting. I
think, for me, the 'thumbs up, thumbs down' model of criticism
is less interesting to read and write than something that wants to
talk about the book not as an object but as an experience, and
as something that has very complicated pleasures that go beyond
admiration or revulsion.

IC: Is there some example where it's shifted and moved and
changed for you?

PS: There's a book I reviewed a while ago by Mohammed Hanif
called *Red Birds,* and I didn't love it. I gave it a pretty mixed
review, but after the review I kept thinking about all the things I
said that didn't work, and why they didn't work. It's not that the
book necessarily changed my notion of what a good book or a
bad book is, but it changed my notion of where I derive pleasure
from a book. The fact that, years later, I'm still thinking about that

book and still thinking about 'Why did he do that? Why did he make that decision? What's in it that's got its hooks in me?' means something. It's very different from books that I can read and love and say, 'Oh, this is fantastic. There's not one lumpy or bumpy sentence in it, the characters are believable, the plot is smooth', and you put it away and forget it. Somehow, these other books, these other experiences, really get their barbs in you, and I'll walk down the street and suddenly wonder about that little odd point of view shift, which I didn't like but I'm still thinking about, it's still part of my material reality in an intense way.

IC: Would you talk a little bit about the process of writing a book review? Just what that process is from the moment you have the book assigned to you to the review?

PS: Isaac, you know very well that my process is a mess. I deeply resent having to answer this question in public. The process is: I'm given a book and I read the book, and then I try to read, in the time allotted, everything else by the writer. I want to read every review they've gotten, every review they have written. I want to read, if I have time, books they are in conversation with, other books in the field. It's just a matter of amassing as much information as I can and as much context as I can—my husband likes to tease me that it also allows me to procrastinate and not write for as long as I can, because I'm in 'research mode'. Writing is so difficult and never gets easier, but when you're researching, you convince yourself you're working. I take notes frantically and put them all into an enormous document and then start to sift through them. Then I read the book again and look at all these pieces, and I try to make a story about what this book means in the context of this writer's career, or if it's a first book, what this writer is in conversation with, what they are writing against.

I don't often know where I'm going. One starts to write out of these fragments and hunches. Martin Amis says that quotation is the critic's evidence. Whenever I have a hunch, or claim, it's incumbent on me to find and produce the evidence.

There are some reviewers and some critics who are very honourable and nervous about being influenced, so they don't read other reviews that the book has gotten, but I try to read every single review. I feel that you can do some sort of recuperative work, you can comment on reviewing in general, for example. It's really interesting, to me, to see in reviews of novels by women, how technical aspects really aren't often discussed; the content is discussed but the form the book takes, these sorts of things are often ignored. So, I think with some of my reviews, I like to have a bit of a corrective function, and draw the attention back to where I think it should be.

IC: Is there a different process for a bigger critical essay than a single book review? You just did a very long piece for *The New Yorker*, 'The Case Against the Trauma Plot',[8] on trauma and trauma literature, which is 5,000 words or so. You talk about a lot of different books and you're not reviewing a book, so I'm curious about that critical essay. Is it the same process of reading everything surrounding it and taking fragmentary notes and getting your quotes lined up? Or, is it that when you move away from a single book to a larger critical idea that your process changes in some way?

---

8   Parul Sehgal, 'The Case Against the Trauma Plot', *The New Yorker*, 27 December 2021.

PS: I think the only difference is that if the piece isn't pegged to a book, there's a chance I've been living with its themes for a bit longer. The trauma piece came out of a class I teach about trauma literature, so I had already done a fair amount of reading. But, no, the process is the same.

IC: Do you have a reader in mind when you're writing? This is something that, I think, feels like, at least with political journalism, a much bigger thing in the last few years. I think there's been an assumption by a lot of people who write for places like *The New Yorker*, that they're only being read by a certain type of reader, politically speaking. I'm curious whether you have a specific type of reader in mind, and whether that's changed over the course of your career?

PS: That's a good question. I don't know if I have a particular reader in mind, but I do know that the sensation of writing for a newspaper is very different from the one I get from writing for a magazine. When I was writing for *The New York Times*, I was writing a weekly column; it was a shorter piece, and embedded in a newspaper. I always wanted to surface what felt new about the book; if it was a novel, if there's something new in technique or approach, if there's something new in this voice, and wanting that to be very central. I always had this feeling when I was writing for the newspaper, of wanting to entrap somebody who has no interest in reading books or reviews. I wanted to trap them in the review, like fly paper.

Writing for a place like *The New Yorker*, I'm having to unlearn the habit of providing a lot of information. I can assume a degree of commitment and curiosity. I don't need a newsy peg or lure.

My questions and concerns can open up a little; I find myself asking broader questions like, 'What does it mean to be a reader now?' I'm wending my way back to your question, I suppose. I don't think of a specific reader, but I do think of the particular set of circumstances in which we're all reading right now. I'm very conscious of all the tabs open on my computer at any minute; I'm very conscious of writing for someone that I think probably also has a million open tabs, open demands, and a crying child or two.

I think my idea of the reader is always somebody who has better things to do. It's about, 'How do I keep you here? How do I keep you with me? I know you want to go do something else. I know you want to check Twitter.' It's having a heightened sense of my own capacity for boredom, and my own sense of having multiple obligations that governs my awareness as I write and try to keep you with me, keep you interested.

IC: I read something you said a long time ago, and, of all the things that I found trying to research this interview, this is the one thing that I was most surprised to hear. You said, 'Taxonomizing has very little to do with how and why people read. It's just the work of criticism I enjoy. Getting close to the text, close to the language.' Do you think that's true?

PS: I think I've probably done a bit more taxonomizing in my reviewing since then. I'm not like a lot of reviewers I love, like James Wood, who are associated with overarching theories of fiction: Here's what fiction should do, and here's what a novel ought to be. I don't think that I have any steady, settled answers for those questions. I do like to look at every book as presenting its own particular and peculiar kinds of problems, and then taking shape around them.

IC: What I was thinking when you said about getting close to the text and to language as sort of the job of criticism, I was curious if there was more to it than that? I feel like a lot of your criticism stems from a passionate desire to express something—whether it's an artistic or political opinion—that is beyond the specifics of the texts themselves.

PS: You're right but I encounter the writer's own artistic and political opinions in the style itself, in the language, in the verbs and rhythms, in the placement of the camera. I think I'm always drawn to those writers for whom style isn't mere filigree (Amis again: 'style is morality').

IC: You keep mentioning Martin Amis. My sense of one of the things he's trying to say in the quotes you're offering or the comments about him you're making, which maybe stem from [George] Orwell, which is this idea that corruptions of language is a sign of, or inevitably leads to, larger corruptions, whether in politics or society or something else. That there's some value to clear prose that makes sense because it's often a sign of clear thoughts and a lack of, say, political lying or something else. Is that something you feel too, or are you making a smaller-scale point about the language?

PS: I think Amis got a lot from Orwell, but I don't think Amis got clear, lucid prose from Orwell. I think with Amis you're talking about somebody who wants an adverb modifying an adverb, and I'm like that too. I don't think that clarity necessarily lends itself to morality, although I understand that argument. I think that the choices you make as a writer, as an artist, bespeak something about how you're looking at your world, your place in it, and the function of fiction or non-fiction. All of which the reader imbibes.

Gertrude Stein says, 'If you enjoy it, you understand it.' I'm fond of this notion and I believe it—that judgement is quick, deep, native, continuous and the readers do it without the critic's interventions. All of us are incredibly gifted and swift readers of people and of texts, and far more sensitive than we give ourselves credit for. The criticism I really like knows that about readers and does not condescend to them.

IC: We haven't talked a lot about the critics you like, other than Martin Amis. Who were the critics that spoke to you most when you started out? Also, who are the critics that speak to you most now? And, as you're answering, does anything occur to you about how that list has changed and why?

PS: I started out really loving Virginia Woolf's criticism, loving Martin Amis, loving Susan Sontag, and I've added a few other people to it. There's the delirious Wayne Koestenbaum; I really admire Pankaj Mishra; I really like poetry critics; I really like critics who write about fields that I don't know very much about; and I tend to actually like critics that can do things I can't or won't do. When I think about Mishra, I think about how deftly he contextualizes fiction—he's always attuned to what this book means or what the success of this writer means in a global context, the global marketplace and global power. I'm not that kind of critic; I'm grateful that he is.

IC: Are there other critics that you like who do not just write about books? Are they doing something that you think is helpful for you as a book critic? And when you read critics from other fields, what is it that you think that they can or don't accomplish that book critics should try to accomplish?

PS: I love dance critics, especially Arlene Croce, who was a writer for *The New Yorker* for many years and wrote about ballet. It was the 1970s, you couldn't go in there with a notepad and take copious notes in the dark. So, what she would do is see a performance and return home and just write about what had stayed with her—what remained, like a fragrance. A few gestures, a few moves, whatever she remembered. It's antithetical to the way book critics work, surrounded by and sifting through mountains of text and evidence. The kind of confidence and authority she possessed to write pieces based on memory, on fleeting impressions, is so impressive, and moving, to me.

I'm not somebody who cares about clothes very much, but I love fashion writing; I love Judith Thurman, who writes for *The New Yorker*; I loved Kennedy Fraser, who wrote for *The New Yorker* a long time ago; and Robin Givhan at *The Washington Post*. What attracts me is the difference, because they're looking at clothes as a way of speaking without language, and I think that when you write about clothes, you always have to write about class and aspiration, all of these things that book critics can sometimes be wary of or pretend to be above.

IC: How do you read like a reviewer? Do you ever get any time to just read like a reader without your reviewing glasses on?

PS: I don't think I can turn it off anymore at this point. I don't think I can read without a pen in my hand. But at the same time,

I don't think I ever read without a pen in my hand. To read like a reviewer, for me, means opening a book and just feeling this sense of heightened alertness—wanting to watch everything as it happens but also trying to empty myself a little bit of what I think those things mean. It means not wanting to move too fast and saying, 'This means that this isn't working', or 'This means that this is wonderful'. I don't want to do that. I want to give the book a really fair shake and I want to be patient. It involves being alert in that sense, but also alert to my own responses.

When I finish the book or, even to some degree, as I'm reading it, when I have a strong reaction to something that's happening, either positive or negative, or wanting to understand what that is about—a little bit not wanting to necessarily believe it or go with it, but open it up a little bit and say, 'What's being triggered?' You become very aware of the borders of your own taste when you read, and I think that part of my job is to just live there. I'm always trying to figure out when something doesn't sit with me or something feels odd or awkward, is it something that I don't know how to read yet? Do I not know the language of this particular book yet? Is this some kind of mulishness on my part, or is this because this is new?

IC: It seems like the upshot of a lot of the things you've said: It's very hard to separate out you being a critic, from you, Parul, as a person. You keep saying, 'I'd be reading like this if it weren't for my job in some way', and that, I guess to some degree, we all get involved in writing and journalism not for the money, but because we like it and care about it in some way. Do you think that's accurate, that the degree to which you as a critic is you as a person, is perhaps greater than it would be if you'd taken some other job?

PS: Maybe, but I also think that criticism is something of a native language for people. I think we're critical creatures. I think we're always trying to order and make sense of what we're seeing.

IC: Due to the financial models of journalism, as a critic you have to publish two to three pieces a week. How does one replenish one's craft when one has to churn out like a machine? Your previous job was churning out a bit like a machine, so I want to ask you that. You also make an interesting point about procrastination. Do you think procrastinating or lingering before sitting down to write can also be understood as a process to fashion your ideas, see how your words fit into places and convey feelings better?

PS: I love the way you are covertly enabling me in my horrible process. To the first question, I know that feeling so well—feeling like a dried-up well, and then being like, 'It's Monday again. I don't have any thoughts.' The only thing I can figure out, which is so simple, is just doing stuff that involves you as a body, not as a mind. And I always felt a little replenished when I got a break from book criticism—to do any other kind of writing or reporting, whether it was a profile, whether it was writing about film or TV, just something that involved a different kind of looking. I think because when you're writing about books, it's so cerebral and argument-based. But no getting around it: procrastination remains my drug of choice, and I always convince myself that I need it, that I need that pressure, I need to feel the pressure of ideas.

I think it's now too late for me. I'm going to take your extremely kind and generous explanation that procrastination is an enshrined part of the process. While I'm twiddling away 'researching', the writing is happening in a chamber of my mind. Let's hope.

IC: Can you talk a little bit about the dilemma South Asian writers, based in the subcontinent, who are writing non-diaspora narratives, run into, whether to legitimize and inevitably simplify complexities or not? Whether to italicize, whether to break up caste in a way that would be unnatural for someone already here? Also, if you can talk about reviewing translations, which is a slightly different thing.

PS: I hate the pressure to make writing, which is and must be specific and local, so legible in these particular ways. As much as possible, I would say resist it, and I do think that there is more of an awareness of what is lost when writers are asked to simplify, flatten and overexplain their characters and their stories, and where they're coming from. I feel hopeful that you don't feel that foot on your neck, because I think it's bad for books and reading in general.

About the reviewing translations question, yes, it's trickier, it is different. What I end up doing is reviewing the book, and then trying, as best as I can, especially if I don't speak the language, to talk about the translation, and to talk about how seamless or awkward it feels. Also, what the challenges of translating a particular book like that could have been. It's really difficult but also really interesting because it forces you to pay even closer attention to the language and knowing that there's a story beyond this—you're getting one version of it. There's a little bit more mystery involved when you're writing about a book in translation.

IC: Another question that I was hoping we could touch on is—how conscious are you of the marketing and commercial implications of reviewing one book over another? What helps you to choose which books to review from the infinite options? Is it always assigned or do you select them yourself? Also, I'm curious when you were at a place like *The New York Times*—a lot of writers feel getting reviewed in *The Times* is the biggest thing that can happen to their book—what do you think about that responsibility?

PS: I think about it a lot, especially because in America, venues for criticism have all but dried up. There used to be a time when any book could be guaranteed a hundred serious reviews in newspapers, and now we have a couple of places left. I balanced it by reviewing books from indie publishers, lots of translations. You have to review some of the big books—our readers will be curious about a new Jonathan Franzen—but there are going to be weeks where you can fulfil your own agenda and bring news of what's happening.

IC: As a South Asian writer, say, are you wary sometimes of pitching reviews for a book whose context is different from yours? Is it important to be familiar with, or part of a specific book's entire previous canon when one goes into a review?

PS: It helps and it's certainly the way that I like to work. I like to feel that I have some grounding, especially because I like to go and review books that I have no credentials for. I want to review everything. I want to review photography, I want to review poetry, and you're able to do that only by doing the homework—by spending time, by grounding yourself to know what's been said about this particular book, or writer and their particular field. You can't always do that pragmatically, especially if you're writing a review for a newspaper or a magazine, if it's just a couple of hundred words. It doesn't even make sense for you to spend that much time. It's really a matter of what the assignment is, what the venue is, and what's the cost-benefit analysis; what makes sense for you.

IC: Have you noticed a general theme to the things you like about the books you review? And, if you sit with a book and open it up and know nothing about the book or the writer, is that an experience that you ever had or miss in some way?

PS: I think it's an experience I try to have with every book. When I'm interested, I want to go and read everything that has been said about this particular writer and what they've done—perhaps, it's a writer I know, and I've read everything else and have my own ideas. The way I frame it to myself is that the culture has particular ideas about this writer, certain things have been said, certain patterns have been noticed, all of this is there, but I want to be blank when I read it. I want to be as open as somebody who has never read this particular writer before, and not let my own impressions, memory and thoughts creep in around the margins. I really want to have that experience of just looking at a book as something fresh and new and different, and allowing it to make that impression on me. And then, in the review, if there's space and time, I'd talk about what sort of ideas and misunderstandings and chatter has accumulated around this particular writer's name and reputation—and some of it is mine too. The book itself demands that of the reviewer.

As for the first question, I like so many different things, but if there's something that is exciting to me, it's books that aren't afraid to take strange shapes and risks. In fiction and in non-fiction, that kind of waywardness is always really interesting to me.

IC: There are obviously a lot of critics who've tried their hand at novels. Is there anyone that you think you would call a great critic and a great novelist? Zadie Smith comes to mind as someone, Virginia Woolf is another. Who else is on that list in your mind, or is it a very short list?

PS: I'm not touching that question! It's designed to get me in trouble. Who are our great critic-novelists? I think, historically, sure, Virginia Woolf is great; Amis has his moments; Randall Jarrell wrote one good novel and great criticism; I guess Elizabeth Hardwick to some degree, if you can call *Sleepless Nights* a novel; D.H. Lawrence wrote great criticism—wacky shit, really strange, but really good.

IC: Unlike his fiction …

PS: Fair enough! I think that there aren't as many 'critic practitioners' today. You do have people that dabble as critics and will write a novel, but in terms of novelists writing great criticism, I think we're in a little bit of a drought.

IC: Well then, to end, if you could send everyone off to read one novel, and one piece or book of criticism, what would it be, and why?

PS: With novels, I would never say that. I'd say read what you want in terms of novels, but in terms of criticism, I can tell you.

There's a great book of criticism called *Seduction and Betrayal* by Elizabeth Hardwick. It's about the great heroines in Western literature, but really it's about power, it's about the domestic, it's about Hardwick's own style. If you want to read a really enthralling kind of criticism that feels like literature in its own right, and gives it a real sense of the stakes of what it means to read fiction that deeply, I highly recommend it.

ABOUT THE
CONTRIBUTORS

Alice Albinia is an award-winning author of fiction and non-fiction. Her books include *Empires of the Indus: The Story of a River*, *Cwen*, which was shortlisted for the Orwell Prize for Political Fiction and Scotland's National Book Awards; and *The Britannias*. She has worked as an editor and journalist, writing for publications including *The Guardian*, *Financial Times* and *National Geographic*. She has taught writing in Orkney for the Islands' Council, at King's College London and the University of Kent.

Deepa Anappara's first novel *Djinn Patrol on the Purple Line* was named as one of the best books of the year by *The New York Times*, *The Washington Post*, *Time* and NPR. It won the Edgar Award for Best Novel, was longlisted for the Women's Prize for Fiction 2020 and shortlisted for the JCB Prize for Literature. It has been translated into over twenty languages. Anappara is the co-editor of *Letters to a Writer of Colour*. Her second novel, *The Last of Earth*, will be published in 2025. She lives in London and teaches creative writing.

Diksha Basu is the internationally bestselling author of the novels *The Windfall* and *Destination Wedding*.

Rahul Bhattacharya is a writer and editor. He is the author of a cricket tour book, *Pundits from Pakistan*, and a novel, *The Sly Company of People Who Care*, winner of the Royal Society of Literature Ondaatje Prize and the Hindu Literary Prize. He lives in Delhi.

Fatima Bhutto was born in Kabul, Afghanistan, and grew up between Syria and Pakistan. She is the author of several books, both fiction and non-fiction. Her debut novel, *The Shadow of the Crescent Moon*, was longlisted for the Baileys Women's Prize for Fiction and the memoir about her father's life and assassination, *Songs of Blood and Sword*, was published to acclaim. Her most recent books are *The Runaways*, a novel, and *New Kings of the World*, a reportage on globalization and popular culture.

Mansi Choksi is a journalist who writes about the intersection of gender, crime, opportunity and pop-culture. Her first book *The Newlyweds*, about love and crime in India, was published in 2022. The *Financial Times* called it 'compelling and heart-breaking' and *The Times*, London, named it 'a staggeringly good work of literary journalism'. The book was the basis of an NPR podcast called 'Love Commandos' which aired in 2023.

Isaac Chotiner is a staff writer at *The New Yorker*, where he is the principal contributor to 'Q. & A.', a series of interviews with public figures in politics, media, books, business, technology, and more.

Sonia Faleiro is the author of *The Good Girls: An Ordinary Killing*, which was nominated for the Royal Society of Literature Ondaatje Prize, the ALCS Gold Dagger for Non-fiction and the Premio

Inge Feltrinelli Award. Her earlier book *Beautiful Thing: Inside the Secret World of Bombay's Dance Bars* was nominated for the Lettre Ulysses Award for the art of reportage. She is the founder of the literary mentorship South Asia Speaks.

V.V. Ganeshananthan is the author of the novels *Brotherless Night* and *Love Marriage*. The former, a New York Times Editors' Choice pick, won the Carol Shields Prize and the Women's Prize for Fiction in 2024.

Roman Gautam is the editor of *Himal Southasian*, a review magazine of politics and culture covering the whole of the South Asia region. He was previously a senior editor at *The Caravan*, a Delhi-based magazine of long-form and investigative journalism.

Vinod Jose edited *The Caravan* from 2009 to 2023. He was educated at Columbia Journalism School, was a Radcliffe Fellow at Harvard University, and has won several national and international awards. His journalism has invited troubles for him: in 2005, his apartment in Delhi was burned down, and in 2021, he was slapped with several sedition cases across India. He is working on a book on Indian political history to be published globally by HarperCollins.

Mira Kamdar, a former member of *The New York Times* Editorial Board writing on international affairs, is the Paris-based author of *Motiba's Tattoos: A Granddaughter's Journey into Her Indian Family's Past*, which won the Washington Book Award and was a Barnes & Noble Discover Great New Writers selection. Her book *Planet India: The Turbulent Rise of the Largest Democracy and the Future of Our World* has been translated into over a dozen languages. She is also the author of *India in the 21st Century* and *80 mots de l'Inde*, a collection of essays originally published as columns in the French weekly *Courrier International*.

Meena Kandasamy is a poet, writer, translator, anti-caste activist and academic. In 2022, she was elected as a Fellow of the Royal Society of Literature and awarded the PEN Hermann Kesten Prize for her writing and work as a 'fearless fighter for democracy, human rights and the free word'. Her latest published work is *Tomorrow Someone Will Arrest You*, a collection of political poetry of the last decade.

Taran N. Khan is the author of *Shadow City: A Woman Walks Kabul*.

Jamil Jan Kochai is the author of *The Haunting of Hajji Hotak and Other Stories*, a winner of the 2023 Aspen Words Literary Prize and a finalist for the 2022 National Book Award. His debut novel *99 Nights in Logar* won the John C. Zacharis First Book Award. His short stories have appeared in *The New Yorker*, The O. Henry Prize Stories and The Best American Short Stories.

Karan Mahajan is the author of *Family Planning*, a finalist for the International Dylan Thomas Prize, and *The Association of Small Bombs*, which was shortlisted for the 2016 National Book Award and was named one of *The New York Times Book Review's* '10 Best Books of 2016'. In 2017, he was selected as one of Granta's Best Young American Novelists. His third novel, *The Complex*, will be released in 2025.

Sanam Maher is the author of *A Woman Like Her: The Short Life of Qandeel Baloch.*

Suketu Mehta is the New York-based author of *Maximum City: Bombay Lost and Found*, which won the Kiriyama Prize and the Hutch Crossword Award, and was a finalist for the 2005 Pulitzer Prize, the Lettre Ulysses Prize, the BBC4 Samuel Johnson Prize, and the Guardian First Book Award. His book about global migration, *This Land Is Our Land*, was published by Farrar Straus & Giroux in June 2019. He is working on a non-fiction book about immigrants in contemporary New York, for which he was awarded a Guggenheim fellowship.

Pankaj Mishra's books include *Age of Anger: A History of the Present, From the Ruins of Empire: The Intellectuals Who Remade Asia* and two novels, the most recent of which is *Run and Hide.*

Mira Nair is an Academy Award–nominated director. Her debut feature, *Salaam Bombay!* (1988) won the Caméra d'Or at Cannes, followed by the groundbreaking *Mississippi Masala* (1991), the Golden Globe and Emmy-winning *Hysterical Blindness* (2001) and the international hit *Monsoon Wedding* (2001), for which she was the first woman to win Venice Film Festival's coveted Golden Lion. She has filmed *The Namesake* (2006), *The Reluctant Fundamentalist* (2012), *Vanity Fair* (2004), *A Suitable Boy* (2020) and *Queen of Katwe* (2016). Her next film is an experimental portrait of Amrita Sher-Gil.

Anuvab Pal is the author of the stage plays *Chaos Theory, The President Is Coming, Life, Love and EBITDA, Fatwa*, and the cult comedy *Loins of Punjab Presents*. He has presented his stand-up comedy special *The Nation Wants to Know* in thirty cities. His BBC stand-up *The Empire* has been seen by six million people worldwide as part of the BBC World Service New Year's Eve Comedy Special and is featured at The V&A Museum in London and on Amazon Prime UK. He's written a sitcom starring Stephen Fry for BBC Radio 2, and a Radio series *Empirical Evidence* with comedian/cricket commentator Andy Zaltzman for BBC Radio 4.

Nilanjana S. Roy is the author of three novels, *Black River*, *The Wildings* and *The Hundred Names of Darkness*, a book of essays on reading, *The Girl Who Ate Books*, and the editor of three anthologies, including *Our Freedoms*. She lives in New Delhi.

Parul Sehgal is a staff writer at *The New Yorker*. Previously, she was a book critic at *The New York Times*, where she also worked as a senior editor and columnist.

Mayukh Sen is the James Beard Award–winning author of *Taste Makers: Seven Immigrant Women Who Revolutionized Food in America* (WW Norton, 2021) and *Love, Queenie: Merle Oberon, Hollywood's First South Asian Star* (WW Norton, 2025). His work has been anthologized in three editions of *The Best American Food Writing*. He teaches journalism at New York University and lives in Brooklyn.

Kamila Shamsie is the author of eight novels, including *Home Fire* which won the Women's Prize for Fiction and was longlisted for the Man Booker Prize. Four of her novels have won awards from the Pakistan Academy of Letters. A Vice President of the

Royal Society of Literature, she grew up in Karachi, and now lives in London and Doha where she is Writer-in-Residence at Georgetown University in Qatar. Her novels have been translated into more than 30 languages.

Taymour Soomro is the author of the novel *Other Names for Love* and the co-editor of the essay collection *Letters to a Writer of Color*. His writing has appeared in *The New Yorker* and *The New York Times*. He has received fellowships from the Wisconsin Institute for Creative Writing, the Sozopol Fiction Seminars and the Bread Loaf Writers Conference. He teaches at the Bennington Writing Seminars.

Samanth Subramanian is a writer and journalist. His most recent book is *A Dominant Character: The Radical Science and Restless Politics of JBS Haldane*.

Mariam Tareen is a writer, teacher and founder of The Writing Room, a platform for aspiring writers. She was a 2022 South Asia Speaks Fellow.

Manjushree Thapa is the author of eight books of literary fiction and non-fiction centred on social and political subjects in Nepal. She also translates Nepali-language literature into English.

Vauhini Vara is the author of *The Immortal King Rao*, a finalist for the Pulitzer Prize, and *This Is Salvaged*. She is also a journalist, writing for *Wired* and others.

HarperCollins _Publishers_ India

At HarperCollins India, we believe in telling the best stories and finding the widest readership for our books in every format possible. We started publishing in 1992; a great deal has changed since then, but what has remained constant is the passion with which our authors write their books, the love with which readers receive them, and the sheer joy and excitement that we as publishers feel in being a part of the publishing process.

Over the years, we've had the pleasure of publishing some of the finest writing from the subcontinent and around the world, including several award-winning titles and some of the biggest bestsellers in India's publishing history. But nothing has meant more to us than the fact that millions of people have read the books we published, and that somewhere, a book of ours might have made a difference.

As we look to the future, we go back to that one word—a word which has been a driving force for us all these years.

Read.

Harper
Collins

HARPER
FICTION

HARPER
NON-FICTION

HARPER
BUSINESS

HarperCollins
Children's Books

HARPER
DESIGN

Harper
Sport

HARPER
PERENNIAL

HARPER
VANTAGE

हार्पर
हिन्दी